Quarterly Essay

Quarterly Essay is published four times a year by Black Inc., an imprint of Schwartz Books Pty Ltd. Publisher: Morry Schwartz.

ISBN 9781760642860 ISSN 1832-0953

Subscriptions – 1 year print & digital (4 issues): $79.95 within Australia incl. GST. Outside Australia $119.95. 2 years print & digital (8 issues): $149.95 within Australia incl. GST. 1 year digital only: $49.95.

Payment may be made by Mastercard or Visa, or by cheque made out to Schwartz Books. Payment includes postage and handling.

To subscribe, fill out and post the subscription card or form inside this issue, or subscribe online:

quarterlyessay.com
subscribe@blackincbooks.com
Phone: 61 3 9486 0288

Correspondence should be addressed to:

The Editor, Quarterly Essay
Level 1, 221 Drummond Street
Carlton VIC 3053 Australia
Phone: 61 3 9486 0288 / Fax: 61 3 9011 6106
Email: quarterlyessay@blackincbooks.com

Editor: Chris Feik. Management: Elisabeth Young. Publicity: Anna Lensky. Design: Guy Mirabella. Assistant Editor: Kirstie Innes-Will. Production Coordinator: Marilyn de Castro. Typesetting: Duncan Blachford.

Printed in Australia by McPherson's Printing Group. The paper used to produce this book comes from wood grown in sustainable forests.

EXIT STRATEGY

Politics after the Pandemic

George Megalogenis

Australia has a justified reputation for avoiding the super-shocks of the twenty-first century. Twice now we have been the exception to the global rule of systems failure. Ours was the only developed economy in the G20 that did not fall into recession during the global financial crisis of 2008–09, and we were one of only a handful of nations to eliminate community transmission of COVID-19 during the pandemic of 2020 and 2021.

Yet our policy ingenuity and social cohesion in the face of existential threats were undermined on both occasions by poor leadership once the immediate crisis passed. Twice now we've seen prime ministers at the peak of their domestic popularity fumble the reform tests they set for themselves.

When Scott Morrison broke his promise to vaccinate Australians by October 2021, voters would have felt a shiver of recognition. The manner of the backdown – not just the fact of it, but the sneaky way it was communicated – echoed Kevin Rudd's politically fatal decision eleven years earlier to walk away from his great moral challenge of climate change.

The Liberal prime minister did not reveal the changes to his program in the formal setting of a press conference. Nor did he issue a statement on his official media site. Morrison waited until a Sunday evening, after the television news bulletins had gone to air and the first editions of the next morning's papers had been printed, to issue a short, carefully worded statement on his Facebook account. "The Government has ... not set, nor has any plans to set new targets for completing first doses," he wrote on 11 April. "While we would like to see these doses completed before the end of the year, it is not possible to set such targets given the many uncertainties involved." Future historians will be confronted by a deliberate gap in the official timeline. They will see the first confident announcement on the prime minister's website last August that Australians would be at the head of the global queue for vaccines. They will see the dissembling as targets were missed, culminating in Morrison's snippy insistence as recently as March that the revised program – at least one jab by October – was on track. But the admission that the exercise had run off the rails will not appear in the official record.

It was too smart by half. The vaccine rollout is the final and most difficult element in our great escape from the pandemic, demanding consistent leadership, public service competence and a high degree of community trust. Morrison, of all people, would know that a late-night post on Facebook, the home territory of anti-vaxxers and conspiracy theorists, risks confidence in the program. Only two months earlier, the prime minister had advised us where not to go for health advice: "Don't go to Facebook to find out about the vaccine. Go to official government websites."

When Rudd shelved his plans for an emissions trading scheme in 2010, he hoped to bury the announcement in the May budget papers. But the plan was foiled by journalist Lenore Taylor, who broke the story in *The Sydney Morning Herald* on 27 April. What the Labor prime minister should have done next was call a press conference at Parliament House to explain his decision. But he doubled down on his strategy of deflection by inviting the media to the Nepean Hospital in Penrith for a discussion of health policy. The local journalists refused to play the game. The first six questions were on climate change, and the long, tortured answers confirmed the futility of the exercise.

Rudd: "Given that international action has been slower than was originally anticipated and given the fact that the Liberal Party has now backflipped completely on this position and therefore the legislation has not been passed – given those two factors, it's very plain that the correct course of action is to extend the implementation date."

Compare with Morrison in 2021: "Now, I've been asked a bit about what our targets are. One of the things about COVID is it writes its own rules. You don't get to set the agenda, you have to be able to respond quickly to when things change. And it's certainly the case over the course of this past year, we've had to deal with a lot of changes."

Rudd and Morrison were claiming to be both hero and innocent victim. They had steered Australia through the respective storms of the GFC and the global pandemic, thereby making us the "envy of the world." But now sinister forces beyond their control had undermined their best intentions.

Rudd did not get away with it. The government "lost the support of around one million voters in just a fortnight," Labor frontbencher Mark Butler wrote in his book *Climate Wars*. "One voter told me in my electorate of Port Adelaide, 'I was never really sold on the whole climate issue, but was willing to back you in anyway – but when you just suddenly dropped the thing because things got too hard, you lost me. I thought you were all piss-weak.'" Within two months, Julia Gillard took Rudd's job. Within four months, Labor was reduced to a minority government. Public satisfaction with democracy had been at a record high when Rudd led Labor into office at the 2007 election. It went into freefall in 2010, after his removal as prime minister, and by decade's end had crashed to its lowest level since the constitutional crisis of the mid-1970s, while trust in government hit an all-time low.

Morrison had risen at the bottom of this long cycle of disillusionment; the fourth prime minister in eight years to claim power through the back door of a party-room coup. He took office in the winter of 2018 with no expectations, and exceeded them when he led his exhausted government to a narrow victory at the May 2019 election. His successful campaign was built around a relentless attack on an unpopular opponent, Bill Shorten, and a caricature of Labor's spending and taxing policies. It was no more outrageous than Labor's own scare campaign against the government in 2016. But Morrison made no attempt to talk up his own agenda. He assumed voters were disengaged, and directed that cynicism at his opponent. Undermining trust in government was a precondition for victory.

The prime minister drove that trust to even deeper lows with his passive and aggressive response to the Black Summer of fires, telling Australians he didn't hold a hose, mate. All the world came to know him as the leader who had snuck off to Hawaii for a family holiday while his country burned. With expectations reset at zero, he exceeded them once more with his handling of the pandemic, only to revert to a point somewhere between the two extremes with the vaccine program. The setback might not hurt Morrison politically while voters remain comfortable with the security blankets of closed borders and economic stimulus. But a third wave of the coronavirus, requiring another extended lockdown, would test the electorate's patience. Either way, Australia is once again in danger of snatching mediocrity from the jaws of achievement.

The key question for this essay is: can Australia restore faith in good government? Are we doomed to repeat the farce of the last decade, when we avoided the worst of the GFC only to succumb to policy gridlock and American-style electoral polarisation in the recovery? Or will the visceral experience of the pandemic allow us to reconceive the political economy of the nation?

Politicians who have only known the open economic model have been forced to provide care, and security against an invisible enemy, using the old tools of intervention. These levers are both familiar and alien at the same time. The closing of borders and the opening of the public purse to support people in lockdown came naturally enough. The difficulty has been in repairing the safety net and restoring public services that were previously entrusted to the market. COVID-19 has demonstrated a wicked genius for exploiting the gaps in the old model, most notably in the management of hotel quarantine for returned travellers, and in aged care, where the lines between private and public, and between the federal and state governments, were blurred.

Between the fires and the plague, Morrison learnt to be a more collaborative leader. He had no choice but to adapt to the realities of federation. The Commonwealth directed the economic response, but the states were responsible for their own health systems. The premiers exercised that authority at critical moments during the crisis, and elevated the standing of both levels of governments as the first and second waves were defeated. But the running of things by the Commonwealth, whether it's the rollout of the vaccine or the safe return of Australians stranded in virus hotspots overseas, remains Morrison's, and our, Achilles heel. While COVID-19 still burns around the globe and Australia remains poised between the elimination of community transmission and another outbreak, there is a still a risk that we slip from the short list of countries to be envied.

In 2020, we boasted the third-lowest death rate among the G20 countries, with only South Korea and China ahead of us, and were grateful that we didn't have a leader like Donald Trump or Boris Johnson, who had neither the humility to heed the advice of experts nor the discipline to hold the line of lockdown. In June 2021, the United States still had the highest death toll in the world, and the UK the highest in Europe. But the perverse incentives of the coronavirus have inspired them to vaccinate their people as quickly as possible. The US is leading the G20, with 41.5 per cent of the population fully vaccinated, while the UK is second, with 39 per cent of the population receiving two jabs. Australia was at the bottom of the table, with just 2.2 per cent fully vaccinated. Even Zimbabwe and Myanmar had higher rates of vaccination at the time of writing.

This essay does not pretend to cover every lesson of the pandemic when the end point remains unknowable. The aim is to identify those parts of the old model that are irredeemably broken, and to provide a new answer to the question of what government should be responsible for in the twenty-first century.

The best place to begin the search for that answer happens to be the United States, where the great new policy experiment of intervention is also underway, with the results to shape the global economy for the remainder of the decade and beyond.

BEFORE AND AFTER NEOLIBERALISM

The United States has reached a historic moment of self-awareness, brought on by pandemic: the model of capitalism authored by Ronald Reagan is over. "Trickle-down economics has never worked," Joe Biden declared in his first address as president to a joint session of Congress in April, "and it is time to grow the economy from the bottom and the middle out." The statement would have been unremarkable if made by an economist. The idea that Reaganomics relied on a confidence trick has been understood in academic circles for some years. But Biden is the first US leader prepared to call neoliberalism's bluff by deliberately increasing the size of government, and paying for it, in part, with higher taxes on companies and individuals.

The cost of Biden's agenda, released within his first 100 days in office, totals US$6 trillion. It has three connected parts. The first, valued at $1.9 trillion and signed into law on his fiftieth day in office, on 11 March, was stimulus for an economy still ravaged by COVID-19. Something on this scale would have been delivered no matter who won the 2020 election. Almost a year earlier, on 27 March 2020, Donald Trump set the record for the largest emergency aid in US history, with a $2-trillion stimulus package, while Congress passed another $900-billion package last December.

An interesting detail for Australia is that Biden's program boosted temporary income support for low- and middle-income earners at precisely the time the Morrison government was withdrawing both the wages subsidy known as JobKeeper and the COVID supplement to the dole known as JobSeeker. The US was lifting families with young children out of poverty and Australia was sending them back into it.

Biden wants to make history with his $2.3-trillion infrastructure plan and his $1.8-trillion families plan. Released within weeks of each other in March and April, they propose a permanent transfer of resources from the private to the public sector. The corporate tax rate is to jump by a third, from 21 per cent to 28 per cent, to help fund investments in buildings, utilities, manufacturing, scientific research and in-home care for the aged and people with disabilities. The top personal tax rate is to rise to 39.6 per cent – back to where it was before Trump cut it to 37 per cent in 2017 – to pay for record spending on education, child and family support. The tax hikes are modest by Australian standards. Even Tony Abbott, the prime minister who tried to impose the deepest cuts on government here in a generation, increased taxes to fund his own promises. He called them levies, but they were the same thing. Where Biden represents a break with the American politics of the past forty years is in his explicit rejection of the notion that government has to shrink.

His education policies are of particular interest to Australians, as successive Coalition governments here have squeezed the funding of public schools and universities. Biden has offered two years of free early education for all American children aged three and four, and two years of free community college after high school. Early learning has been a particular blind spot for both countries. The United States has the lowest rates of attendance in the developed world for children aged three and four, while Australia's rates are below average for both years. Only 40 per cent of American children and 65 per cent of Australian children aged three attend early learning classes, compared to 100 per cent in Britain and France, and more than 90 per cent in most other European countries. In our own region, South Korea is at 92 per cent and New Zealand at 88 per cent. Australian policy-makers are not used to the Americans setting their safety net above ours. But it remains to be seen whether Biden provokes a race to the top on education here. The Coalition would need to abandon, or at least pause, its project to tilt the education budget towards private schools, which began with the first Howard government in 1996. And Labor would have to be prepared to fight an election on the issue.

Both sides will have noted that Biden's agenda is popular. When polled, almost two-thirds of US voters agreed with tax increases for the wealthy. The same proportion supported the centrepiece of the plan for free education. Also, just over half (51 per cent) agreed with the statement that "trickle-down economics have never worked in America," while only

26 per cent disagreed. "Any way you slice it, all of Biden's economic proposals – and his mechanisms for paying for them – are popular," according to FiveThirtyEight's election analyst Nathaniel Rakich.

Biden appears to be an unlikely man to lead an economic revolution. A career politician, he had erred on the side of compromise since his election to the US Senate in 1972, age twenty-nine. But Reagan, a former Hollywood actor and governor of California, was seen as an improbable agent for change in his day. What both men have in common is that they assumed power in the teeth of an economic crisis. The US has held six presidential elections during a recession: in 1920, 1932, 1960, 1980, 2008 and 2020. The White House changed hands each time. The transformative elections for the American economic model were in 1932 and 1980. That places Biden in the sweet spot for reform, based on the precedents of Roosevelt and Reagan.

Franklin D. Roosevelt took office in 1933, with the unregulated model of capitalism discredited by the Great Depression. Almost one in four US citizens (24 per cent) were out of work. "Our greatest primary task is to put people to work," he said in his inauguration speech in January 1933. "It can be accomplished *in part* [my emphasis] by direct recruiting by the Government itself, treating the task as we would treat the emergency of a war, but at the same time, through this employment, accomplishing greatly needed projects to stimulate and reorganize the use of our natural resources."

Roosevelt's New Deal program, which introduced social security to America in 1935, did not end the crisis. Unemployment remained above 10 per cent for the remainder of the decade; full employment was not achieved until the United States entered World War II. But it provided the first draft of the model that dominated economic thinking for the next half-century, with the federal government as an active player in the economy. The cycle of influence from America to Australia operated with a time lag of about a decade. We didn't become New Deal–style nation-builders until 1943, when the tide had turned in the Pacific and John Curtin's Labor government began planning the post-war reconstruction.

The apotheosis of the New Deal in the United States was Lyndon Johnson's Great Society program in the mid-1960s, which introduced the Medicare and Medicaid health programs for the aged, disabled and low-income earners, and included a significant expansion in funding for education. Gough Whitlam's program happened to be even more ambitious. He laid the groundwork for a superior safety net; one that proved to be more resistant to the sharper edges of neoliberalism than its American counterpart. Whitlam gave us Medibank, the first draft of our universal health-care system, as well as free tertiary education. But his timing was off. Labor took office in 1972 on the brink of the global economic storm of "stagflation" – rising unemployment and inflation – and as the orthodoxy was turning towards deregulation of markets.

Whitlam increased the size of the federal government by a third, but his dismissal in 1975 did not shift things immediately. The new prime minister, Malcom Fraser, was a protectionist, and did not shrink the government, even though he abolished Medibank.

The distance between Reagan's election in November 1980 and Australia's embrace of the open model was just two and a half years, the distance between an era-defining boom and bust that brought down Fraser's government and returned Labor to power under Bob Hawke in March 1983. It created an unusual dynamic between the originators of neoliberalism and their pragmatic disciples in Australia.

Reagan defined the US government as the culprit for stagflation. The problem was not just excess spending or bad policy but the public servants who formed the backbone of the government. "In this present crisis," he said in his inaugural address in January 1981, "government is not the solution to our problem; government is the problem ... It is time to check and reverse the growth of government, which shows signs of having grown beyond the consent of the governed."

He drew the false equivalence between the household budget and the federal budget. "You and I, as individuals, can, by borrowing, live beyond our means, but for only a limited period of time. Why, then, should we think that collectively, as a nation, we are not bound by that same limitation?" Despite this, under Reagan the federal deficit actually grew. He cut taxes, as promised, but he also increased the size of government. Australia, on the other hand, cut taxes and achieved a series of budget surpluses in the 1980s under Labor. The Americans never lived up to their rhetoric of small government, but we took them literally.

Was it worth it? Recently, David Hope and Julian Limberg at the London School of Economics looked at the record of eighteen advanced economies, including Australia's, and found that "major tax cuts for the rich over the past 50 years have pushed up inequality but have had no significant effects on economic growth or unemployment." Among the major reforms they investigated were the Reagan tax cuts of 1982 and Paul Keating's in 1987. Both delivered a sharp increase in the share of national income going to the top 1 per cent of earners, but without any appreciable boost to economic activity. "These findings shed new light on a debate that has long divided policymakers, with one side claiming higher taxes on the rich could raise revenue and reduce inequality, and the other arguing that low taxes on the rich are the best route to wider economic prosperity. The data suggests that low taxes on the rich bring economies little benefit, and this suggests there is a strong economic case for raising taxes on the rich to help repair public finances following the pandemic."

Readers of my previous Quarterly Essay, *Balancing Act*, might recall that I ran a similar but more narrowly focused exercise looking at the generous tax cuts John Howard's government delivered between 2005 and 2007, which saw many higher-income earners pay the marginal tax rate of 30 cents in the dollar meant for average earners.

> John Howard and [treasurer] Peter Costello did not consciously set out to make the income-tax system an agent for inequality. They thought the reverse would occur: by reducing the burden on the top, everyone would want to climb the ladder. No one doubted the theory in the government or the bureaucracy. Tax cuts were

> supposed to reward effort, and to encourage people to save and invest ... One thing is clear, though: [these] tax cuts made Australia less fair.
>
> We know this now because of a fascinating study undertaken by Nicolas Herault and Francisco Azpitarte ... They looked at the period of our greatest prosperity, from the late 1990s to the eve of the global financial crisis, and found that, measured in take-home pay, inequality increased. The Howard government tax cuts were not the only reason, but they were a significant factor. "We find that the direct effect of tax-transfer policy reforms accounts for approximately half of the observed increase in income inequality over this period," they wrote.

The power of neoliberalism was never in its observance by conservatives but its effect on the other party. While Reagan did not live up to his ideology, Bill Clinton adopted it as his own and delivered the death blow to Roosevelt's New Deal. The Democrat took office in 1993, in the aftermath of a mild US recession. He had campaigned on a promise to "end welfare as we know it." He turned that slogan into legislation in 1996, by eliminating the federal entitlement program that Roosevelt introduced sixty-one years earlier and replacing it with a state-based system of temporary welfare, with work requirements.

Robert Reich, then Clinton's labour secretary, and other members of the cabinet were appalled by the policy. "It was too punitive, we said, subjecting poor Americans to deep and abiding poverty," Reich wrote. "But Clinton's political advisers warned that unless he went along, he would jeopardize his reelection [in 1996]. That was the end of welfare as we knew it. As Clinton boasted in his State of the Union address to Congress that year: 'The era of big government is over.'"

It was conventional wisdom at the time, both in the US and Australia, that welfare was too generous. The two Dons, Watson and Russell, respectively the speechwriter and chief of staff to Paul Keating, had suggested a Labor crackdown on welfare before the 1996 federal election might "bamboozle" Opposition leader John Howard. "Ten minutes of talkback told anyone prepared to listen that Paul Keating would not lose votes by declaring that Labor's social wage was not designed to reward sloth equally with industry and ambition," Watson wrote in *Recollections of a Bleeding Heart*. But Keating wasn't interested in a last-minute pivot to the right.

The Republicans doubled down on tax cuts under the presidency of George W. Bush, creating the worst of both worlds: a compromised revenue base, collecting even less tax than Reagan did in the 1980s, and a broken safety net. Bush delivered a budget deficit in each of his eight years in office, whereas the Howard government boasted surpluses in seven of those eight years.

While the American economy was booming and the number of people on welfare kept falling, it was easy to misread Clinton's tough love as a form of trickle-up economics, giving people the nudge they needed to lift themselves out of poverty. But the savings were illusory. The welfare budget exploded again during the global financial crisis and the pandemic.

The word "government" did not appear at all in Biden's inaugural address, but restoring public trust in the institution is central to his mission. He used his first televised address to the American people – on 11 March, timed to coincide with the first anniversary of the WHO declaration of a pandemic – to talk up the role of government. "We need to remember, the government isn't some foreign force in a distant capital. No, it's us, all of us, we the people. For you and I, that America thrives when we give our hearts, when we turn our hands to common purpose."

This was music to Reich's ears. He heard the comment as a repudiation of Clinton. "As a senator, Biden supported Clinton's 1996 welfare restrictions, as did most Americans. What happened between then and now? Three big things." The first was the COVID-19 recession, "which revealed the harsh consequences of most Americans living paycheck to paycheck." The second was Trump, who "obliterated concerns about government giveaways" with his tax cuts for the top end in 2018 and his stimulus cheque for all in 2020. The third was the extent to which Biden's plan lifted the standard of living for lower and middle-income earners. "The political lesson is that today's Democrats ... can gain political majorities by raising the wages of both middle class and poor voters. The economic lesson is that Reaganomics is officially dead ... Bidenomics is exactly the reverse: Give cash to the bottom two-thirds and their purchasing power will drive growth for everyone."

We had already worked this out in Australia. The combination of wage subsidies and a doubling of the dole payment ensured that our economy had recovered all the jobs it lost during lockdown by April 2021, as Biden was putting his stimulus into the US economy.

The journey to Biden's epiphany began twelve years earlier, when he was Barack Obama's vice-president. Obama took office in January 2009, with the US in its deepest recession since the Great Depression. Expectations were impossibly high. Obama immediately went to work on stimulus for the economy. His plan was worth $787 billion: less than half the value of either the Trump or Biden packages. The following month, Obama announced a bailout of the auto industry. By year's end, the federal deficit had hit 9.8 per cent of GDP, the highest level since 1945. Each momentous decision gave Obama more leverage in the American economy than any president since Roosevelt.

But the intriguing thing is what didn't happen next. Obama did not take the opportunity to reimagine the model beyond the introduction of health-care reform. He finished his second term in 2017 with spending at the same level as Reagan had twenty years earlier. Keynesian in the crisis, pro-market in the recovery, Obama left the economy in reasonable shape: unemployment was lower than under Reagan. Once again, a Democrat had proven to be the more efficient neoliberal.

But the divisions in American society only deepened on his watch. Middle-class incomes stagnated and did not return to pre-GFC levels until the end of his second term. And life expectancy for the white working class without a college degree fell for three years in a row between 2015 and 2017, a damning statistic for the world's largest economy. Obama inherited these problems from Reagan, Clinton and Bush, and could not fix them while he operated within the old model. As Princeton University economist Anne Case notes in her groundbreaking research with Angus Deaton on the "deaths of despair," the wages of working men without college degrees have been in decline since 1979. Deaton, a Nobel Prize–winning economist, said the short-term shocks of recession do not explain lower life expectancy in the US. "It has to be this long-term drip of losing opportunities and losing meaning and structure in life."

Looking back, Biden believes that Obama was naive in assuming that stimulus would sell itself. "You know, the confidence in the American … government has been plummeting since the late '60s to what it is now," Biden told a meeting of the House Democratic caucus in March this year. "And many of you remember that in 2009, we expended a lot of political capital – [House speaker] Nancy [Pelosi] and I and others – in the *Recovery Act*. [The] economists told us we literally saved America from a depression. But we didn't adequately explain what we had done. Barack was so modest, he didn't want to take, as he said, a 'victory lap'. I kept saying, 'Tell people what we did.' He said, 'We don't have time. I'm not going to take a victory lap.' And we paid a price for it, ironically, for that humility."

Others in the Democrat leadership saw the size of stimulus as the problem rather than the marketing of it. More broadly, the problem was what Obama *hadn't* done.

"We're not going to make the mistake of 2008 and 2009 and do such a small, measly proposal that it won't get us out of the mess that we are in right now," Senate majority leader Chuck Schumer said of Obama's $787-billion package. "We've had a weak, limp economy over the last ten years. We've got to do a lot better than that, to help the American people, give them hope, the American optimism that is so important … [otherwise] they turn to a demagogue, a bigot like Donald Trump."

The American backlash to the GFC was part of a wider trend that predated the arrival of Trump and his explicit platform of bigotry and isolationism. Politics shifted to the right in every English-speaking country, and throughout Europe. Conservatives took office in Britain in 2010, and in Australia in 2013, while conservative incumbents in Canada and New Zealand were re-elected. Obama was the electoral outlier, securing a second term in 2012, although by then his power was constrained by the scorched-earth obstruction of a Republican-controlled Senate.

Neoliberalism avoided a reckoning after the GFC because governments were spooked by the deficits they had run up in the crisis. It made intuitive sense for incumbents to rebuild fiscal buffers for the next shock, and for oppositions to carp about debt and deficit disasters. In the UK, where neoliberalism had found its first global apostle with the election of Margaret Thatcher's conservative government back in 1979, David Cameron thought he had nailed the slogan for the next phase of the model: austerity.

"The age of irresponsibility is giving way to the age of austerity," the then opposition leader declared in 2009. "Now, some people say: let's get through the recession, let's get through the election, we can keep on spending more, keep on borrowing more, and deal with the debt crisis later. Wrong – seriously wrong. The alternative to dealing with the debt crisis now is mounting debt, higher interest rates and a weaker economy. Unless we deal with this debt crisis, we risk becoming once again the sick man of Europe."

The slogan won him an election and, along with like-minded governments in Europe, Cameron and his chancellor of the exchequer, George Osborne, proceeded to slash spending before the economy had reached the cruising speed of recovery. The European Union, of which the UK was then a proud member, slipped into a second recession at the end of 2011, barely two years after the GFC had ended.

Cameron had promised to spare the National Health Service from the slings and arrows of austerity. But the public health system was nonetheless squeezed by successive governments, including Labour's before him. England's hospitals lost 32,000 beds over ten years – roughly the same number as had to be found in a matter of months to cope with the first wave of the coronavirus in 2020.

This is the reason why Biden's agenda to repair safety nets and to rebuild economies "from the bottom and middle out" has global resonance – it addresses the mistakes his peers made during the lost decade between the GFC and the pandemic.

Boris Johnson began preparing the ground for a UK version of a New Deal before Biden became president. "This has been a disaster, let's not mince our words," the British prime minister said of the pandemic in June 2020. "This has been an absolute nightmare for the country and the country has gone through a profound shock. But in those moments you have the opportunity to change and to do things better. We really want to build back better, to do things differently, to invest in infrastructure, transport, broadband – you name it." What he wouldn't do was "go back to what people called austerity, it wasn't actually austerity but people called it austerity, and I think that would be a mistake. I think this is the moment for a Rooseveltian approach to the UK."

It is almost too neat: Johnson as the anti-Thatcher to Biden's anti-Reagan (and anti-Clinton), especially when Johnson was guilty of Trumpian mismanagement of the virus itself. But Johnson and Biden have taken the first step to restoring trust in their governments with their vaccine programs. And they have established a joint ticket for action on climate change.

The question for Australia is whether we will adapt our model to the new consensus for a more active government or continue to muddle through with our version of the old model – a generous safety net, deficit spending to support households and encourage business through a crisis – but with a passive government in recovery. That depends on whether the recession we had in 2020 will prompt a reckoning. If it does, will Scott Morrison's government have the imagination for the job?

Recession used to creep up on Australia. It did not announce itself in a singular, unambiguous global shock but in increments of missed signals. Months would pass before the fall was confirmed in the rear-view mirror of economic statistics. By then it was almost too late to prevent a hard landing.

Once consumers closed their wallets, and businesses began laying off staff, the victims were easy to identify. The burden of retrenchment would be borne by blue-collar workers in manufacturing and construction. Around four out of the five jobs that disappeared in the deep recessions of the mid-1970s, the early 1980s and the early 1990s belonged to men who had been working full-time. Women suffered a disproportionate share of the job losses just once before the lockdown of 2020, in the credit-squeeze recession of 1961.

The political scars of recession remain visible long after recovery. The credit squeeze confirmed the power of the economy to humble even the most dominant leader. The government of Robert Menzies lost fifteen seats at the 1961 election; if one more had changed hands, Labor's Arthur Calwell would have been prime minister and Australia would have avoided the Vietnam War alongside Harold Wilson's United Kingdom. The Whitlam recession in 1974–75 broke the post-war promise that every person who wanted a job could have one. The Fraser–Howard recession in 1982–83 terminated the old economic model of protection. And the Hawke–Keating recession in 1990–91, the first of the open economy, exposed the fault lines which have shaped our politics ever since, between young and old, between city and country, and between the cosmopolitan south-east and the parochial north and west.

Each episode is worth revisiting to understand the unique character of the health-induced recession of 2020. I will focus first on the relationship between politicians and the public service. A common feature of the economic crises of the twentieth century was the breakdown in trust within the system, which condemned Australians to higher rates of unemployment and lower standards of living than were necessary. I want to show how we finally learnt to cope with economic shocks by conquering our institutional fear of intervention, and how the conservative side of politics, backed by a partisan media, almost wrecked the new model in the decade leading up to the pandemic.

*

The post-war recessions followed the same grim script. They had in common a prime minister and treasurer who did not see the crash coming and a Treasury department that compounded its own errors of forecasting with advice against stimulus to prop up the economy.

"This was not something that the Australian Treasury had dreamt up," former Treasury secretary Ken Henry told me. It was time-honoured orthodoxy.

> The academic consensus around fiscal policy was basically: "It's too hard to use." There are so many lags, recognition lags, implementation lags [that] there's no point trying to avoid an even deeper recession by active fiscal policy. You will probably just make matters worse. [But] once you've decided that government can only make things worse, you've already made up your mind, haven't you? That the best thing to do is sit on your hands and let the private sector work it out.

Treasury believed that the so-called automatic stabilisers in the federal budget, which slashed tax collections and boosted expenditure on unemployment and other social benefits as economic activity slowed, would be sufficient to support people in hard times. Additional government spending over and above that mechanical process was thought to do more harm than good because the funds would reach the economy when they were no longer required, in recovery. The theory of tough love was applied regardless of the economic model. The department gave this advice to the governments of Menzies, Whitlam and Fraser – when officials fixed the exchange rate, interest rates, wages and the cost of imports – and to the government of Hawke and Keating – when three of those prices were determined by the market, while the Reserve Bank set interest rates independently. Viewed in retrospect, it is extraordinary that our finest economic minds would make the same prideful mistake from recession to recession because they didn't trust the government of the day to spend money in a crisis. The irony is that Treasury did not recognise the flaw in its textbook approach until it found a prime minister in Bob Hawke and a treasurer in Paul Keating who were willing to follow its uncompromising advice to the full in the final recession of the twentieth century. Without that epiphany, it is hard to imagine Australia avoiding the global financial crisis in 2008–09, or executing a near-perfect lockdown and recovery during the pandemic of 2020 and 2021.

To be fair, the first iteration of the Treasury line was drawn by necessity, because the conservative politicians they served were prone to indecision. Harold Holt, the treasurer in the Menzies government, was so slow to accept the official advice to cut spending and raise interest rates during the boom of 1960 that the Reserve Bank threatened to use the formal provisions for resolving disputes with the government by tabling its advice in the parliament. Holt eventually agreed to do what Treasury wanted. But the credit squeeze, as it came to be known, was applied after the economy had begun slowing, turning what might have been a soft landing into a crash in 1961.

A humbler public service might have accepted part of the blame. But it was easier for economists to believe that the worst of the crisis could have been avoided if only the politicians had done what they were told in the first place. The credit squeeze was a deep recession when measured by lost production, but mild on the measure that matters most: jobs. The unemployment rate peaked at 3.2 per cent in 1962, but returned to below 2 per cent by 1964, where it stayed for the remainder of the decade.

Treasury's sense of intellectual and moral superiority was reinforced by the recessions of the mid-1970s and early 1980s, when unemployment and inflation exploded in tandem. The department famously fell out with both sides of politics, as first Whitlam's government then Fraser's ignored the advice for moderation. It was at this point that the political system started to view recession from the wrong end of the telescope. Because the spending came too late to alter the trajectory of the Whitlam or Fraser recessions, spending was assumed to have contributed to both, thereby confusing cause and effect. Treasury had a vested interest in this interpretation. By shifting attention to the budget deficit, the department absolved itself of any responsibility for failing to anticipate the recession.

The department had not encountered a prime minister like Gough Whitlam before, with an ambitious social reform agenda of his own, informed by experts outside the bureaucracy. Determined not be patronised by the public service, Whitlam and his ministers guaranteed that they would be treated like children in return. The tone of the relationship can be seen in extraordinary private discussion between the Treasury secretary, Sir Frederick Wheeler, and Whitlam over the loans affair. Sir Fredrick wanted the prime minister to kill the plan by energy minister Rex Connor to bypass Treasury and borrow money directly from the newly rich Arab oil-exporting nations to fund grandiose infrastructure programs in Australia.

"Shut up," Whitlam snapped. "I've heard everything."

Sir Frederick replied: "Prime Minister, you will listen to me. I am drawing to your attention facts, your ignorance of which will bring you down."

The loans affairs had no practical consequence for the economy because Whitlam shut down the scheme in 1975 before a dollar was borrowed. The real damage had occurred in the previous year's budget. Treasury, the Reserve Bank and Whitlam's key advisers H.C. "Nugget" Coombs and Fred Gruen had all pushed for spending cuts and increased taxes to fight inflation. Initially, Whitlam was open to the idea, but he soon lost interest. This was all the encouragement his ministers needed to go rogue. Egged on by deputy prime minister Jim Cairns, they indulged in the greatest spending spree since the war. Neither Whitlam nor treasurer Frank Crean was prepared to rein them in.

Programs that Labor had waited a generation to introduce were crammed into a single document. Total spending rose by a staggering 32 per cent. After inflation was subtracted, the real increase was 20 per cent, which symbolically amounted to almost a percentage point for every year Labor had been out of office between 1949 and 1972. The economy had already tumbled into recession before the budget was tabled in the parliament in September 1974. Given the lags between announcement and delivery, it is unlikely that the money arrived in time to cushion the landing. Employers laid off almost 80,000 workers between May 1974 and February 1975.

A significant portion of the new spending was devoted to expanding the role of the federal government into areas previously left to the states. For instance, the 1974 budget was the first to carry the full cost of Commonwealth funding for universities and colleges.

Treasury registered its disapproval by refusing to write the introduction to the budget. The economic twist to this story is that Whitlam ultimately accepted the Treasury line, just like Menzies and Holt had before him. Whitlam allowed interest rates to be raised and offered an olive branch to the department by appointing the well-regarded Bill Hayden as treasurer in 1975.

Whitlam had two abiding economic regrets. He should have made Hayden treasurer in his first year, not his last. And he thought his credit squeeze of higher interest rates was "begun too late; it was too severe; it lasted too long." The unemployment rate had been 2.1 per cent when Labor had been re-elected in May 1974. By November 1975, it had more than doubled, to 5.4 per cent. Unlike the Holt credit squeeze, which ended with a return to full employment, the unemployment rate kept drifting higher in recovery, and was still above 6 per cent by decade's end.

Fraser preached small-government conservatism three and a half years before Margaret Thatcher took office in Britain and five years before Ronald Reagan was elected US president. In practice, though, Fraser was an old-school Keynesian, and he shared Whitlam's suspicion of Treasury, even though the department had leaked to the Opposition during the loans affair. Fraser split the department to create a Department of Finance, which might offer a second line of economic advice to government.

(Malcolm Fraser told me that he never found out the identity of the Treasury officer who had been leaking to his Treasury spokesman, Phillip Lynch. But Lynch did share the alias. "In earlier days [in the Menzies government], for some reason, which I don't really understand, if somebody wanted to speak to Bob Santamaria, you'd ring up a number and ask for 'Mr Williams'. Well, Mr Williams was the pseudonym of the Treasury source also.")

When the next crisis struck in 1982, Fraser pushed for a big-spending budget, over the objection of Treasury and his own treasurer, John Howard. It came too late to save the economy from a stagflation recession, in which both unemployment and inflation crossed 10 per cent for the first and only time on record.

Treasury usually had the final word in those days. As the electorate disposed of first the Whitlam and then the Fraser regimes, the department made sure that each new government understood how reckless its predecessor had been. The settling of scores reached its apotheosis after the 1983 election, when the Treasury secretary, John Stone, informed Hawke and Keating that Fraser and Howard had destroyed the integrity of the budget and misled voters about the true size of the deficit.

The department would balance the ledger of shame after the 1996 election, when less emotive advice was delivered to the incoming Howard government that the Keating government had left the budget in deficit.

The new government, whatever its ideological leanings, was always grateful for the documentary evidence that its opponent had been a hopeless economic manager. The next election campaign and the one after that practically wrote themselves. "Where's the money really coming from, Mr Howard?" "Labor's black hole."

But this cycle of crash and recrimination, of political instability and bureaucratic payback, dumbed down the economic debate. The lesson of recession was reduced to a political slogan – debt and deficit – and the idea formed, almost by default, that the primary role of government was the pursuit of a budget surplus regardless of the state of the economy.

When the relationship between Treasury and government was at its most functional and creative in the reform decade of the 1980s, the department thought that a succession of budget surpluses would reduce the current account deficit, which is the gap between what we buy and sell to the rest of the world and the income Australian residents earn from the rest of the world less what they pay to it. Treasurer Keating obliged, with three surpluses between 1987–88 and 1989–90. The current account deficit was supposed to narrow at this point, because the government was no longer borrowing new money to fund its deficits. Henry explained:

> What happened was that as fiscal policy got under control, the private sector felt more confident and so we had this investment boom. But the government at the time was committed to getting the current account deficit under control. If you've got an investment boom on your hands, the current account deficit widens. It doesn't narrow, as the government was telling people it was going to do. Ultimately all instruments were brought to bear on the current account deficit, including monetary policy.

Keating and the Reserve Bank were at cross-purposes. He pressed for higher interest rates to curb demand for imports, while the bank, which did not believe in the twin-deficits theory, was trying to kill inflation. Watching different datasets, each with their own time lags, the government, Treasury and Reserve Bank conspired to push rates too high, and leave them there for too long.

Soon after Keating conceded that Australia had slipped into a recession "we had to have," he switched the rationale for tough love from the current account to inflation. And he would not let go of his surplus, just as Treasury asked. The budget actually remained in balance over the twelve months that the economy contracted. More than 240,000 workers lost their jobs in that financial year of fiscal discipline, while the unemployment rate jumped from 7.1 per cent in July 1990 to 9.5 per cent by June 1991.

As Keating observed to me, "It took so long to produce the surplus, a structural surplus, I don't mean a cheap one, but one where we cut the long-term structural outlays, I don't think anyone in the government wanted to touch it, you know. It was like a piece of gold."

"But it wasn't the appropriate response at the time," I said.

Keating: "In hindsight, we could have had fiscal policy more accommodating as well, and particularly as monetary policy was still unaccommodating – that is, with interest rates falling, but too slowly. But it's very hard to pick the depths of these things, you know."

Keating abandoned the Treasury line following his first failed leadership challenge against Hawke, in June 1991. He remade himself on the back bench as an interventionist, ready to answer the call from the Labor caucus to kickstart the recovery. Hawke tried to steer a middle path between Keating's newfound faith in stimulus and Opposition leader John Hewson's radical "Fightback!" program, while he waited in vain for news from the Australian Bureau of Statistics that the economy had turned the corner.

Unemployment had reached 10.5 per cent when Keating ousted Hawke at the second attempt in December 1991, and would peak at 11.2 per cent a year later. Keating went to work on an economic revival plan he dubbed "One Nation." Featuring personal tax cuts, handouts for families and investment in infrastructure, it was framed with one eye to recovery and the other to the election due in March 1993.

"The government at the time stopped listening to the Treasury," Henry said. "Which is something that we had not anticipated. The Australian Treasury had seen itself for good reason as the premier economic advisory unit of government. It had established itself in that position over a long period of time and in the second half of the 1980s it was advising government with no rival anywhere, including [the Reserve Bank] in Martin Place, simply no rival anywhere. And through its unwillingness to offer sensible advice to government in the early 1990s recession it dealt itself out of the policy advising game. Now, this was bad for the institution, but it was also bad for the country. After all, if the economy is in recession, if it's in crisis, you really do want your best economic advisers on the team. You actually do want them in the room."

Treasury should have recognised that with unemployment at a post-war high, it was "politically impossible for a government to sit on its hands and do nothing. The truth is it can do something and it's obviously the case that the Australian population expected the government to do something. People were losing their jobs and so Prime Minister Keating now decided that whatever Treasury is saying, it's now time for the government to act."

The department realised its mistake more than a decade after it made it, following a secret internal review conducted in 2004. The soul-searching had been prompted, in part, by an observation from Martin Parkinson, Henry's deputy, at a top-level meeting that year. "Look around the room," Parkinson whispered to his boss. "You and I are the only people who were here during the [last] recession."

A critical element of the exercise was the examination of both lanes of Keating's One Nation program: the cash payments to households, which arrived within weeks of their announcement; and the government's infrastructure spending, which took years to reach the economy.

"What happened in the 1990s was that yes, the infrastructure projects were eventually identified and yes, the spending did start, but the spending really got underway in 1994, 1995, 1996, 1997, and by then, of course, the economy was growing very, very strongly anyway. These measures that were developed in 1992 turned out to be adding fuel to an already strongly growing economy." In other words, spending can do more harm than good if the government pulls that lever *too late*. But the review did establish the case for a simpler form of stimulus. "We decided that if a government ever found itself in the position of wanting to respond with the budget to weakness in the economy then the best thing to do would be to get money, cash in the hands of Australian households, as quickly as you could do it."

At the time of Treasury's epiphany, there was no prospect the advice would be needed. The economy had been growing for thirteen years, and Australia was just about to catch the dual wave of a China-led mining and migration boom. Treasurer Peter Costello had already secured six budget surpluses in seven years and was preparing to clear all Commonwealth debt.

What Ken Henry and his colleagues could not have known was that the next recession would come without a time-lag. They would not have to play the twentieth-century guessing game of picking the turning point in the cycle, because the transmission from shock to recession was almost instantaneous. Every rich nation knew from the moment the US investment bank Lehman Brothers collapsed in September 2008 and the global financial system froze that their economy would contract in the December quarter that year.

This made it easier to accept the need for intervention. Knowing that one quarter was already a write-off, and that it was nobody's fault, meant they could concentrate on defending the next. In the past, governments would wait until the economy had shrunk for two consecutive quarters before conceding a recession was underway. It was an arbitrary measure, and one economists did not take seriously. But it had an unintended benefit during the GFC. The Rudd government suddenly had time on its side. It had three months to engineer a soft landing, which it could declare with the resumption of growth in the following quarter. Henry's advice to Kevin Rudd to "go early, go hard, go households" was calibrated with this outcome in mind. The $10 billion in cash handouts announced in October and delivered in December would hit the real economy in the March quarter of 2009.

The GFC inverted the relationship between Treasury and the government. The call to spend in a crisis was initiated by public servants, not politicians. The advice was received by a prime minister raised on the false certainty of surplus budgets, who had based his election victory on the promise that he would be more economically conservative than John Howard. "This reckless spending must stop," had been Rudd's catch-cry.

It took him a while to admit publicly that the GFC had changed the rules. Privately, Rudd understood that the price of intervention would be an immediate and dramatic swing into deficit. When Henry suggested the cash handout should be $5 billion, Rudd told him to double it so that people would be in no doubt the government was asking them to spend it. A smaller package of measures was announced in December, followed by an infrastructure statement in February 2009.

On paper, the school building and home insulation programs were small enough to have no bearing on the temperature of the general economy, or on the budget bottom line. They posed no obvious risk of overheating the recovery or blowing out the deficit even further. We know they created jobs in the short term, because the construction sector laid off 6 per cent of its workforce in 2012, the year after the school buildings program wound up. But the expenditure was impossible to defend politically, let alone morally, after four young men lost their lives between October 2009 and February 2010 during the chaotic rollout of the home insulation program. Tragedy was almost unavoidable given the scheme was conceived and delivered in haste, via a largely unregulated industry, by a federal government that no longer had any corporate memory of running things. The chair of the royal commission into the program, Ian Hanger, found that the deaths of Matthew Fuller, Reuben Barnes, Marcus Wilson and Mitchell Sweeney "would, and should, not have occurred had the HIP been properly designed and implemented."

Rudd abruptly cancelled the program after the fourth fatality. He hoped that would make the headlines go away: a duck-and-run ploy he would repeat with climate change policy two months later, in April. But the admission of policy failure on the cheapest part of the government's stimulus program only encouraged Opposition leader Tony Abbott to step up his attack on the entire exercise. By undermining the stimulus, Abbott was able to deny the government any credit for the great escape in the first place.

While Abbott was right about the pink batts scheme, there was no economic basis for his wider argument that the government had spent too much, or that the GFC was somehow a phoney crisis. The stimulus was one of the four domestic factors that kept the economy growing, alongside rapid cuts in interest rates, a well-regulated banking sector and strong population growth through migration. The external gift of China's own stimulus also helped. Opinions will differ on the magnitude and order of importance. But if you remove the Rudd government's stimulus from the equation, then Australia almost certainly joins the rest of the developed world in recession in 2008–09. (China's own spending, which reignited our mining boom, could not have covered the income gap if that initial $10-billion payment to households had not been made. Nor would it have saved the construction sector if the government hadn't "wasted" all that money on school halls.)

Australia's achievement can be appreciated through the counter-examples of the United States and the United Kingdom, the ally and the mother country we no longer look up to. The US economy contracted by 3.9 per cent during the depth of the GFC in 2008–09, and the unemployment rate peaked at 10 per cent. The British economy collapsed by 5.9 per cent, while unemployment reached 8 per cent. Our economy grew by 1.9 per cent and our unemployment rate remained below 6 per cent. It is why we still call this episode the GFC when the rest of the world knows it as the Great Recession. The US response, in particular, was handicapped by the pressing need to bail out financial institutions, which chewed up funds that might otherwise have been directed to households as cash stimulus.

In our region, South Korea avoided a second quarter of contraction, but its economy was still 1.1 per cent smaller over the twelve months of the GFC. New Zealand, on the other hand, had slipped into recession before the GFC started and stayed there. National prime minister John Key eschewed stimulus for old-school neoliberalism, cutting personal taxes and increasing the rate of the goods and services tax. He told New Zealanders he couldn't stop a global recession. "[But] we can use this time to transform the economy to make us stronger so that when the world starts growing again we can be running faster than other countries we compete with." He said the approach taken by Australia and the US was risky, because it would "saddle future generations with an enormous amount of debt that then they have to repay; there is actually a limit to what governments can do."

If Key was right, New Zealand would have recovered faster than Australia from the second half of 2009. Instead, Australia outran New Zealand for the next four years.

The Rudd government didn't lose its way because of its economic policies – they were as good as anyone's during the GFC and its immediate aftermath. The problem was the absence of sustained advocacy. It was a variation of the political naivety Joe Biden diagnosed in Barack Obama. Rudd lacked the patience to explain his successes, and was quick to shift blame when forced on the defensive. His ambitions were too large and his attention span too short to stay on the same topic long enough for the electorate to absorb Labor's agenda. His mind was always racing ahead to the next challenge. All Abbott had to do in response to the torrent of words from the prime minister was repeat three focus-group-tested earworms. Debt and deficit disaster. A great big new tax on everything. Stop the boats.

The problem with Abbott's reply wasn't its querulous tone, or its shameless lack of content. As the third Opposition in just over a year, and with Rudd still enjoying a rock-star personal approval rating, the choice to run scare campaigns on the stimulus, climate change and border protection made sense politically. The two smaller-l Liberals before him, Malcolm Turnbull and Brendan Nelson, couldn't touch Rudd or his government. They had engaged on Labor's terms, on the detail of government policy, and it had made no impression on the opinion polls.

The problem was that Abbott came to believe his own exaggerations, and governed as he campaigned, by yelling. Abbott took two elections to claim power. The last politician to do that from Opposition had been Gough Whitlam. But where the Labor leader used those years in the wilderness to hone his program and prepare the public for reform, Abbott nursed grudges on behalf of a narrow, but electorally decisive constituency fed up with change. Where Whitlam was met with a contemptuous and inward-looking public service, Abbott had the advantage of a world-class bureaucracy which had helped Australia survive the greatest economic shock since the Depression.

Abbott swaggered into office in September 2013, determined to erase six years of Labor policies and the public servants who had worked on them. He had just three departmental secretaries in his sights – half the number Howard sacked after the 1996 election. All had advised on climate change, which for Abbott made them fair game. But the first name on the hit-list happened to be Martin Parkinson, the head of the Treasury. He had been the inaugural secretary of the Department of Climate Change and Energy Efficiency after the 2007 election, before succeeding Henry at the Treasury in 2011. No incoming government had sacked the Treasury secretary before, and it was apparent that Abbott hadn't thought through the consequences of breaching this final frontier of public service independence. First, there was the 2014 budget to prepare. Second, Australia was hosting the G20 meeting in Brisbane at the end of that year. Remove Parkinson before either of those tasks was completed, and the new secretary and his team would be starting from scratch.

Parkinson received notice of his removal after being summoned to a meeting with the head of the Department of Prime Minister and Cabinet, Ian Watt. It was a Saturday afternoon, at the end of the first week of the new government. Abbott didn't even bother to inform his treasurer, Joe Hockey. The weekend passed without a word from his minister, so Parkinson called Hockey's chief of staff, Grant Lovett, on the Monday. Lovett hadn't been told either, which was clear when he asked Parkinson how his weekend went. "Shithouse," he replied. "You bastards sacked me." A few minutes later, Hockey was on the line. "He had no idea this was going to happen," Parkinson told author Marian Wilkinson. "He was clearly upset. In fact, it was a combination of upset and furious. And he went in to bat for me." A compromise was reached which kept Parkinson in his position until the G20, before his exit in December 2014.

*

There is a sliding door for Australia with Tony Abbott's name on it. If we'd passed all the way through it, with a health system undermined by spending cuts and a Treasury compromised by partisanship, our experience of the pandemic would have been closer to that of the United Kingdom, if not the United States.

The Abbott government was elected at the midpoint of a global turn to a disruptive brand of conservatism, between David Cameron's breakthrough in the UK in 2010 after thirteen years of Labour rule and Donald Trump's triumph in the United States in 2016. Abbott's belligerent style of governing anticipated Trump's. Four years before Trump rode a golden escalator to the lobby of the New York tower that bore his name to announce that he would run for president, Abbott, then still Opposition leader, addressed a protest rally on the lawns of Parliament House. Flanked by supporters with signs that read "Ditch the witch" and "JuLiar, Bob Brown's Bitch," Abbott chanced on one of the decade's great political secrets: vulgarity was the new shortcut to power. Misogyny didn't disqualify him from office. Against Australia's first female prime minister it increased his chances of victory by switching a fraction of Labor's blue-collar male voting base to the Coalition.

He chanced on another insight. In the decade between the global financial crisis and the pandemic, it didn't matter what an Opposition party said on economic policy. The traditional media were unable or unwilling to subject an Opposition to the same level of scrutiny as before, because they no longer had sufficient numbers on the reporting floor. The rise of digital media added another barrier to scrutiny.

For example, at my old paper, *The Australian*, there was a clear step-change in the treatment of Abbott compared to previous Opposition leaders. John Howard can vouch for that: *The Australian*, along with the rest of the media, nitpicked his tax policies during the 1987 campaign, and print's judgment that they didn't add up influenced the television and radio coverage. In 1993, John Hewson was treated like an alternative prime minister, with every dollar attached to his Fightback! programs subjected to the same level of analysis as a federal budget. Howard, in his second stint as Opposition leader, narrowed the policy difference with Keating's government, yet we still gave him a hard time. In 2007, as Rudd mimicked Howard's small-target campaign of 1996, agreeing to around 90 per cent of what the government proposed, we were relentless in posing the same questions to the Labor leader as we did to the prime minister on issues such as middle-class welfare. The very fact of such scrutiny ensured that when Australians changed their government, the incoming prime minister was already tethered to some form of policy reality, whether his agenda was declared or hidden.

Abbott didn't need to explain himself. He could go to work every day as Opposition leader confident that he wouldn't face equivalent questions about his policies to those being demanded of the Rudd government's stimulus program. I am not alleging bias, nor am I interested in engaging the culture warriors. My interest is in the operating environment and how it shaped Abbott's brief time in office, and the dangers it posed for good government. Employers like mine at *The Australian* responded to the challenges of falling print circulation – and the shortened attention span of media consumers who swapped from paper to smartphone – by dialling up the commentary at the expense of old-school journalism. It inevitably shifted the slant of everyone's coverage towards those who barracked for a living. Those who supported Abbott cheered him on, while those who couldn't stand the man tried to out-yell him. There was little room in this new media space for analysis of policy.

When Abbott become Opposition leader in December 2009, the media had already shed 40,000 jobs over the previous three years. A further 10,000 disappeared by the time he became prime minister in September 2013. The total losses amounted to more than a fifth of our entire workforce. We had fewer people working in the media than in real estate, mining or the arts.

Abbott skated through the 2010 and 2013 campaigns with a magic pudding program of lower taxes and increased spending. He was asking voters to throw out a Labor government, in part because it couldn't balance the budget, yet his policies were guaranteed to widen the deficit. It was in his interests to leave some wriggle room, as Howard had in 1996, and Bob Hawke had before him in 1983, for the inevitable budget repair after the election. But without sustained scrutiny beforehand, he was never forced to fine-tune his pitch. On the eve of the election, when asked a cursory question about funding for public broadcasting, Abbott assured voters there would be "no cuts to education, no cuts to health, no change to pensions, no change to the GST and no cuts to the ABC or SBS."

He knew he would have to break that promise, but he thought he would get away with it. The Coalition's polling suggested that voters would tolerate the reversal of Abbott's unfunded commitments, most notably his paid parental leave scheme, which was skewed to families at the top of the income ladder. What the incoming prime minister and his advisers didn't seem to register was that Australians were in no mood for deeper cuts to the safety net.

Joe Hockey was careful to avoid using the term "austerity" to describe the sacrifices he was asking of Australians in the government's first budget. "The age of entitlement is over," the treasurer said. "It has to be replaced, not with an age of austerity, but with an age of opportunity." But the ideology was unmistakable. Hockey reached back to the foundational argument of Reaganism that government was the problem. "A smaller, less interfering government won't need as many public servants. 16,500 staff will leave over the next three years without compromising frontline services."

Previous Liberal leaders had tried to make the case for smaller government – Hewson in 1993, and Howard in 1987 – and lost winnable elections for their troubles. On both occasions, Labor actually increased its majority, leaving little room for misinterpretation of the result. The vote-switcher in each campaign was Medicare, the universal public health system. The Coalition wanted to wind it back in favour of a US-style safety net for the poor and the aged, leaving middle Australia with incentives to take out private health cover.

Howard read those elections as the final word on Medicare. He had told me when he was prime minister: "We had to modify our position on Medicare – I did do that quite deliberately. I was against Medicare years ago [but] I came to the conclusion after the '93 election that the public liked Medicare, the public were too welded on to Medicare."

Abbott had been a health minister in Howard's government, and with nineteen years' experience in parliament before becoming prime minister himself, one would expect he knew enough not to play with this particular match. But he couldn't resist. Among the spending cuts and higher taxes Hockey announced on budget night in 2014 was a $7 co-payment for visits to the GP and for out-of-hospital imaging and pathology services.

The operating environment that shielded Abbott in opposition could not protect him from the backlash that followed. No matter how hard his supporters in the media typed and talked, the feedback on the news websites and the calls to radio stations were overwhelmingly about the breach of trust. Abbott didn't make the case to tamper with the safety net before the election. On the contrary, he had explicitly ruled it out. On election night, he accepted the honour of leading Australia with the catch-cry that the grown-ups were back in charge. His would be "a government that says what it means, and means what it says, a government of no surprises and no excuses."

No one could have foreseen it then, but Abbott had accidentally protected Australia from the experiment of austerity. The budget stalled in the Senate, and as voters ousted first-term Coalition governments in Victoria and Queensland, Abbott's colleagues concluded that he would lead them to a landslide defeat at the next federal election.

When the Liberal party room finally gave up on Abbott in September 2015, just short of his second anniversary as prime minister, they replaced him with a politician vowing to restore Cabinet government. One of Malcolm Turnbull's first acts as prime minister was to bring back the public servant Abbott had made an example of. Martin Parkinson returned to the bureaucracy at its very apex, as secretary of the Department of Prime Minister and Cabinet. The institutional memory chain to the GFC and the recession of the early 1990s had been restored. Australia was ready, without knowing it, for the shock of the pandemic.

THE RESPONSE

As the coronavirus launched its silent war on Australia in January 2020, Josh Frydenberg, the third treasurer in a six-year-old Coalition government, was counting the cost of the Black Summer bushfires. He had one thing on his mind as the Treasury department provided an update on the economy and the budget: would he lose his prized surplus?

Frydenberg recounts the briefing, inserting the bad news first. The economy, Treasury told him, was slowing. "We felt that those areas where the bushfires had hit would have an impact on the economy, particularly in tourism," he tells me. "And you also had Sydney covered in smoke, and the ability of people to work was being inhibited." His own office in Parliament House carried a suffocating reminder of the fires still burning along the east coast of Australia. The smoke had invaded the building, forcing staff to tape up their windows for respite. The last of the megablazes was just about to erupt in the nearby Orroral Valley, south of Canberra, prompting the declaration of a state of emergency for the nation's capital. Ahead were the floods and hailstorms.

Treasury wasn't forecasting a bushfire recession. The worst case was that the economy would contract in the March quarter only and bounce back in the June quarter. Nevertheless, a "negative quarter" carried political as well as economic risks. The last Liberal treasurer to face one was Peter Costello, for the December quarter of 2000, following the introduction of the GST. The shock of that news, which arrived in March 2001, sent the government's polling into freefall and prompted an election-year spending spree from John Howard, which left the budget with a small deficit.

Now Frydenberg reflects on the good news he received in that late-January briefing. After weighing the slower economy, and the $2 billion the government had already allocated for bushfire relief, "Treasury's advice to me was that we were still on track for surplus." The fires had not disturbed his worldview, because, based on those numbers, government could still provide assistance without blowing the budget.

I interviewed the federal treasurer at the end of 2020, at his new electorate office in Camberwell, in Melbourne's east. His reflections on a momentous year of fire and plague, of recession and recovery, provide a fascinating first draft of the response to the pandemic from the perspective of the person pulling the economic levers. I was especially interested in Frydenberg's relationship with the Treasury: the advice he received, and how it helped convert him to the new theory of intervention in those critical weeks in March, when the government moved from a mindset of modest stimulus to a historic package of life support for the economy.

Like most members of his political generation, Frydenberg was convinced that the role of government was to nurture the private sector. He had studied economics and law at Monash University, and completed a masters of philosophy at Oxford and a masters of public administration at Harvard. He served a political apprenticeship as an adviser in the Howard government from 1999 to 2004, before getting a real job in the private sector as a director of Deutsche Bank, based in Melbourne, from 2005 to 2009.

His first speech to parliament, in 2010, as the newly elected member of Robert Menzies' old seat of Kooyong, was a mix of neoliberalism and traditional Liberal values. He was pro-market, but also pro-education. "My vision is to achieve what Menzies termed 'civilised capitalism,' unleashing the power of the individual and his enterprise while always providing a safety net for those who despite their best efforts are unable to cope. These are my motivations, my cause and my way, and they are not negotiable." He cited Margaret Thatcher's great putdown of socialism: "that you eventually run out of other people's money." "Thatcher's nemesis was socialism; ours is bigger and bigger government. My goal is to ensure that government learns to live within its means."

But there was one area of Australian life where he wanted more government spending: higher education.

> Much of Australia's future depends on opportunities created by research and teaching in our universities and the quality of training in our vocational sector. The funding of our tertiary institutions

> needs review. We must do better than funding them at below the OECD average. To underfund these institutions is self-defeating because the harvest of intellectual property generated by them can be the source of our prosperity in the knowledge economy of the future.

Neither value would survive contact with the coronavirus. By necessity, Frydenberg became a big spender. And his colleagues didn't share his old enthusiasm for the university sector. This left the pandemic intervention compromised by the lines that were deliberately drawn to keep the universities, and their international students, outside the safety net.

*

The pursuit of surplus had become an obsession for the Coalition. It was meant to give the Morrison government purpose in its third term, after the leadership churn and the policy divisions of the Abbott and Turnbull years. But the fallout from Hockey's 2014 budget meant that spending cuts were out of the question. Without savings on the expenditure side of the budget, the surplus could only come through bracket creep, as inflation pushed workers into paying higher rates of tax. But even that was proving elusive, as wages growth had fallen to record lows under the Coalition.

The upshot, after five (essentially housekeeping) budgets, was that government expenditure crept to an even higher level under the Coalition, even though the spending record of the Rudd and Gillard governments included the stimulus during the global financial crisis. There is an irony here. If the Coalition had got its way and secured a surplus through cuts to the safety net, the economy, still bruised by the GFC, would have slowed to a crawl. The deficits it accepted for political reasons delivered a form of stimulus by default. They kept the unemployment rate between 5 and 6 per cent, although they could not return it to the pre-GFC low of 4 per cent.

Towards the end of February, Frydenberg flew to Riyadh, in Saudi Arabia, for the G20 meeting of finance ministers and central bank governors. It was here that he first sensed the coming storm. "[I] took note of the presentations of the Singaporeans and South Koreans to the ministerial forum, and they both explained how significant the hit on their economies was from the virus. My radar was up. The Singaporeans, who run pretty disciplined budgets, said that they were going run a deficit. Up to this point [based on Treasury advice] I was still pretty confident of delivering a surplus."

On his return home, it was becoming increasingly clear that a global recession was looming, and that its source would be unlike any other. All previous post-war recessions had their epicentre in the United States, the world's largest economy. This one would start in China, the world's largest trading partner. The data that caught everyone's attention in Treasury was released on 29 February: China's manufacturing production index had crashed by 14.3 per cent, the largest on record, "and well below market expectations."

Then came a flashback to simpler times. The national accounts for the December quarter were released on 4 March, and they showed that the economy grew despite the bushfires. None of that mattered now.

Treasury had begun working on a stimulus package straight after the Saudi Arabia trip. Mindful that they were about to step into tricky political terrain, the department's secretary, Steven Kennedy, walked Frydenberg and his ministerial colleagues in the Expenditure Review Committee through the history of the GFC. "At ERC, this was the benefit of having Steven Kennedy as the secretary who had worked closely with the Rudd government during the GFC. He talked about the importance of not redesigning, or building new programs, but using existing systems."

Kennedy updated Treasury's epiphany from the early-1990s recession: the importance of getting cash into people's hands and the danger of relying on infrastructure projects. In a nutshell, the advice said: You should deliver stimulus through existing payment channels. But forget about inventing new programs such as the pink batts scheme.

Steven Kennedy was the fourth Treasury secretary in six years, reflecting the turnover of prime ministers and treasurers in that period. He joined the public service in 1992 as a cadet for the Australian Bureau of Statistics, before moving across to Treasury. When the department war-gamed recession in 2004, he was the general manager of its domestic economic division. His immediate boss was Martin Parkinson.

Public servants who have worked with both men joke about the differences in style between Kennedy and his predecessors. Parkinson, and before him Henry, were cut from the old God cloth of Treasury secretary. Their intellects could be intimidating, one colleague observed. Politicians on both sides found them arrogant, whether they meant to come across that way or not. Kennedy has their intellect but not their ego, one source observes.

Coalition ministers got to know Kennedy through his previous role as secretary of the Department of Infrastructure, Transport, Cities and Regional Development between 2017 and 2019. That appointment, made when Turnbull was prime minister and facilitated by Parkinson, proved to be prescient. When Parkinson retired after the 2019 election, Morrison tapped the then Treasury secretary Phil Gaetjens to take over at Prime Minister and Cabinet, and moved Kennedy to Treasury. Without realising it, Morrison ensured that one of the smartest people in the public service would be in the room when the Coalition needed to ditch two generations of ideological baggage. To appreciate Kennedy's value, consider a plausible alternative. If Treasury had a debt-and-deficit warrior in charge when Australia went into lockdown in March 2020, we might not have had a wage subsidy. Remove that original piece of policy thinking from the pandemic response, and the economy might not have recovered as quickly.

The Rudd government had multiple buffers to deploy during the GFC. It inherited a budget that had been in surplus for seven years, and no net debt, while the Reserve Bank had interest rates it could slash. Those buffers had not been restored by 2020. The budget had been in deficit for twelve years. As each year's shortfall had to be funded by borrowing, the accumulated debt made for embarrassing reading for the Coalition. Labor had left just $200 billion in net Commonwealth debt in 2013–14. The Coalition had pushed that figure towards $400 billion in just six years. Meanwhile, the Reserve Bank had its primary instrument blunted by fellow central banks in the United States and Europe, which had driven official interest rates to near zero during the GFC. The bank had little choice but to eventually fall in line. On the eve of the pandemic, Australia's rate was at a record low of just 0.75 per cent.

On paper, there was no room to move. But our debt was low by international standards. We had borrowed only half as much as the G20 average in the decade between the GFC and the pandemic. The Americans had pushed their government debt to 109 per cent of gross domestic product, the UK debt was 85 per cent of GDP, and the German debt was at 60 per cent of GDP. Australia's gross government debt was 45 per cent. That net Commonwealth debt number, which looked so scary and incompetent when expressed in hundreds of billions of dollars, was actually less than 20 per cent of GDP.

The Reserve Bank had the consolation of an interest rate above zero, which meant it could offer one more cut before resorting to "unconventional monetary policy." Among the options were buying private-sector assets, which some people call "printing money," although banknotes are not actually printed as part of the transaction. The central banks of the United States and Europe had already played that hand during the GFC.

The RBA made a conventional play on 3 March, reducing the interest rate to 0.5 per cent, while the government prepared its first stimulus package. Treasury designed the principles based on the lessons of the GFC. Payments would use existing systems. They would be temporary, targeted and could be dialled up or extended as needed. "Everything was working towards the 12 March package, but we were open to other ones," Frydenberg says. But the virus was spreading faster than the government could make its announcements.

That first package assumed the economy would remain open, and that the crisis could be managed with fewer dollars than Rudd had given to households in October 2008. Pensioners received a one-off payment of

$750. Rudd gave them $1400. Where Labor directed most of its first stimulus package to families and individuals, business was at the front of the queue for the Morrison government's "targeted stimulus package."

The following morning, Morrison had his first meeting of the National Cabinet, made up of premiers and chief ministers, in Sydney. Kennedy gave them a briefing on the economy. He and the governor of the Reserve Bank, Philip Lowe, quickly realised that the measures they had drawn up between them – the government's stimulus and the reduced interest rate – were not just too small, they were addressing the wrong problem. The health restrictions being recommended by the chief medical officer, Dr Brendan Murphy, while modest compared to what followed, meant there was no point trying to promote activity when the economy was being shut down. Where Rudd had put money in people's hands and told them to shop as an act of patriotic duty, Morrison would be paying them to stay home: a form of national sick leave to fight the coronavirus. The cost of supporting people in a lockdown would be many times what any previous government had spent trying to sustain spending in a recession.

Kennedy told the Senate committee investigating the response to COVID-19: "It was very apparent to me immediately that we were moving, perhaps even more quickly than I anticipated, towards changes that would affect the Australian economy over and above even what we anticipated in that first response."

Preparations for the second package had already begun. The gap between the Morrison government's first and second responses to the pandemic would be just ten days, with a third, containing the JobKeeper initiative, to come eight days after that. All three packages would be announced in March 2020. Interest rates were cut twice in the same month. That second reduction to a new record low of 0.25 per cent came after an emergency meeting of the RBA board on 19 March. The cut was the least interesting part of the statement. The news was in the switch to unconventional monetary policy. Lowe said the bank would buy government bonds to force down longer-term interest rates, and offer financial institutions up to

$90 billion in funds at a fixed rate of 0.25 per cent, so they could provide cheap loans to small and medium-sized businesses. He also confirmed that the bank was no longer fighting the old war of inflation first and had shifted its priority to jobs. "The Board will not increase the cash rate target until progress is being made towards full employment and it is confident that inflation will be sustainably within the 2–3 per cent target band."

The pursuit of full employment had not been government policy since Whitlam's day, and it was extraordinary to see the purists at Martin Place leading the revival after four long decades of deregulation and globalisation. In effect, the Reserve Bank had become an interventionist without an obvious lever. It couldn't cut interest rates much further without going to zero. The stimulus was in the signal it gave the market that the rate would not rise for at least the next three years, and that the Bank would cover any borrowings the government made to fund relief for households and businesses.

This new stance effectively passed the baton from the Reserve Bank to Treasury, returning Australia to a version of the 1980s, when the economic department located in Canberra's parliamentary triangle had more influence on government than the central bank in Sydney's CBD. The RBA had drawn its authority from defeating inflation in the early 1990s, containing it during the mining boom in the early 2000s, and keeping the arteries of finance flowing during the GFC. But it had failed to deliver its inflation target of 2 to 3 per cent since 2014. Now it was yielding primacy as economic manager in a crisis to the Treasury.

The language of the second government package reflected the new interventionist advice. It was a "support" package, to "cushion the economic impact of the coronavirus and help build a bridge to recovery." Released on 22 March, it was almost four times the value of the first one: $66.1 billion compared to $17.6 billion. Once again, business was granted priority, with an increased cash-flow payment. A further $750 was given to pensioners, at a cost of $3.9 billion. This was consistent with the Treasury formula for dialling up existing payments as the circumstances demanded.

So was the introduction of a new temporary handout, which the government dubbed the "coronavirus supplement." At $550 a fortnight, it was available to anyone already on the dole, youth allowance, parenting payment, farm household allowance or special benefit. It would run at the full rate for just the six hardest months of the national lockdown before being tapered back. For a government about to turn a promised surplus in 2019–20 into a deficit of $85 billion, it could easily be mistaken for just another bullet point of spending.

But it was radical and inspired policy-making on the run. That $550 a fortnight almost doubled the value of the old Newstart payment to $1117.50. The eligibility criteria were so loose that practically anyone who didn't have a job could claim the supersized dole, and with the economy being shut down there was no point asking the new entrants to the safety net to prove they were looking for work. It was a universal income by another name, temporary, not targeted and entirely unexpected from a Coalition government. Barely six years earlier, Joe Hockey's horror budget demanded that people aged under thirty wait six months before claiming Newstart, while those under twenty-five already on Newstart would be moved to the cheaper (for the government) Youth Allowance. The Senate killed that plan at the time. Now the ghost of that ideology was being buried alongside it. The number of people receiving the supersized dole, renamed JobSeeker, more than doubled from 725,000 in February to 1.464 million by May. Provision was made in the budget to hire 5000 extra public servants to handle the workload.

Kennedy advised that the safety net should be strengthened first before the government considered a broader wage subsidy scheme. He told them that such a scheme was needed to keep workers attached to their employer, even if they worked no hours during lockdown itself. Otherwise, millions more would go on JobSeeker, and the government would have trouble reconnecting them to their old jobs once the lockdown ended. Burned into the collective memory of Treasury and the Reserve Bank was the lesson of the early-1990s recession. The unemployment rate had the same properties as the coronavirus. Left unchecked, the line in the graph would explode in a matter of months, then take years to flatten.

Frydenberg had a video conference with Treasury officers to finalise the support package that went for eight hours. At one point, he asked a deputy secretary what coffee they were drinking. "It's not coffee, it's wine," was the reply.

The support package of Sunday, 22 March, was undermined by an argument at National Cabinet on the same day, and by the government's inexplicable failure to anticipate that, on the following morning, the newly unemployed would line up at every Centrelink office in the country.

The blow-up at National Cabinet was the first tangible sign that the pandemic was rewriting the rules of the federation. The Commonwealth had the financial power, but the states and territories would be the ones enforcing the lockdown. They ran their local health and education systems, and police forces. In the event of a disagreement, the states and territories would go their own way.

Morrison's instinct from the outset was to chart a middle course between the needs of the health system and the economy. He took the virus seriously, unlike Trump or Johnson. Nevertheless, he wanted to keep as many businesses open as possible, and would sweat the detail of each lockdown proposal. Hairdressers and barbers, for example, would soon be glued to their televisions and tablets trying to make sense of the PM's decision allowing them to stay open while also maintaining "strict social distancing" from their customers under the "four square metres per person" rule and "no more than thirty minutes and preferably less" for each appointment

In New Zealand, Jacinda Ardern, the Labour prime minister of a minority government, was about to order the toughest possible lockdown, with the goal of eliminating community transmission before the economy was reopened. Morrison was in the "bend the curve" club of global leaders, who wanted to use a relatively softer lockdown to reduce the spread while also ensuring the hospital system wasn't overwhelmed with patients. The economy would reopen once the infection rate was reduced to a manageable level. He aimed to take the community slowly through each stage of lockdown, from two to three but preferably not four, which is where New Zealand would start.

Ardern had all the powers at her disposal, without state leaders to haggle with, or an upper house to check her legislation. Morrison had three Labor premiers, two Labor chief ministers and three Liberal premiers across the table. Each, in turn, had their own chief health officer. By 22 March, it was clear there were two schools of thought: the Commonwealth's approach of slowing transmission, with a gradual increase in restrictions on the community; and Victoria's eradication strategy, which recommended a prompt move to a stage three lockdown, leaving only essential business open. What Morrison did not anticipate was that Victorian Labor premier Daniel Andrews and NSW Liberal premier Gladys Berejiklian had already grown weary of the prime minister's prevarication. Morrison had clung to Dr Murphy's advice that it was safe to leave schools open. With the greatest respect, the premiers knew that was nonsense and that parents had already voted with their feet, pulling their children out before the end of term. Morrison had also underestimated the bad blood that remained from the Black Summer of bushfires, when he had publicly attacked NSW ministers, and his office briefed against the premier. Howard had had to tell him to stop.

Morrison began the morning of Sunday, 22 March, spruiking the $66.1-billion support package, with its JobSeeker centrepiece. But as he spoke to the media in Canberra, the Victorian and NSW governments were leaking details of their plan to close all non-essential services, including schools. The three bickered all though the day, while Australians cleared the supermarket shelves and raided the bottle shops for lockdown supplies. Morrison emerged for a second press conference after 9 pm to assure Australians that the National Cabinet remained unified, as he announced a new round of closures to apply from Monday. Schools remained open for now. But they would be shut before the end of the coming week.

Having learnt nothing from the bushfires, people close to Morrison resumed the backgrounding. I'll just quote two passages from reports at the time because they mark the moment when the federation buckled.

The Australian's national affairs editor, Simon Benson, wrote:

> Scott Morrison managed to walk the states back from the brink following clear and direct medical and health advice that much of what they were proposing was not only unnecessary but absurd. All leaders signed up to the national cabinet for a reason. It was meant to provide a unified position on a national crisis. Instead the premiers wet the bed and went it alone. This was a major breakdown in policy response and communication. The net effect of this is critical. People will lose trust in governments to manage the crisis. The NSW government is arguably already at this stage.

The Age and *The Sydney Morning Herald* reported:

> All sides are now claiming they are happy with the national cabinet despite the conflicting signals on Sunday. One leader [said] that Sunday night's national cabinet was the "most effective, well chaired and agreeable" meeting yet.
>
> "The idea that there's a rift or a disagreement just isn't right," he said. "Andrews and Gladys shat themselves and went out on their own. Other premiers had to pull them into line. To blame Morrison on this would be totally unfair."
>
> But the big two states believe they will have to go their own way on some issues to combat the virus. "We very much support the national cabinet but we have to make practical decisions about what is happening on the ground in NSW and that might be different to the other states," said one NSW source. "NSW has a very unique set of circumstances, we are not Tasmania. We are the epicentre (of the first wave of infections) and when we need to take action, we have to do that."

As the health response moved inexorably to a more stringent lockdown, Treasury gave Frydenberg two scenarios for the economy: bad and diabolical. The advice on 24 March was that the economy would contract 10–12 per cent in the June quarter. But "if restrictions were increased further, then GDP could fall by 24 per cent in the June quarter," he says.

Tasmania had been the first state to impose its own hard border, on 19 March, locking itself off from the mainland. Australia closed its borders to the rest of the world at 9 pm on the next day. On the 24th, a ban was placed on Australians travelling overseas. By the 26th, the borders of Western Australia, South Australia, the Northern Territory and Queensland were effectively closed, while Victoria kept pressing the Commonwealth to accept the inevitability of a stage three national lockdown.

That day, Frydenberg had an extended meeting with Morrison and finance minister Mathias Cormann to discuss the wage subsidy. Kennedy and Treasury deputy secretary Jenny Wilkinson joined on video. Ambition for the scheme was expanding in direct proportion to the rise in community panic. But Morrison had one proviso: he didn't want the British scheme, which proposed covering up to 80 per cent of workers' wages.

Frydenberg talked again with Morrison and told him he would come back with a range of costings. He also spoke at length to his mentor and old boss John Howard on the phone. Frydenberg underlined the advice from the former prime minister and treasurer in a note he wrote to himself: "In times of crises, there are no ideological constraints."

One advantage Morrison and Frydenberg had over Kevin Rudd and his treasurer Wayne Swan was data. The advances in technology since 2008 meant that government no longer had to wait for the review of official statistics to see where the economy might be heading. Information could be pulled in real time, from the Australian Taxation Office, the banks and retailers. The ATO's single-touch payroll system for employers proved invaluable in designing the JobKeeper payment. It ticked the box for an existing payment system, while also providing the government with a frightening but relevant reading on the state of the jobs market. David Gruen, who was a senior Treasury officer during the GFC and another alumnus of Martin Parkinson's macroeconomic group, was now in charge of the Australian Bureau of Statistics. He explained the difference in information available between the two crises as "chalk and cheese." The ATO payroll data gave him almost instantaneous access to the decisions of employers affecting 10 million workers. What those numbers showed proved to be invaluable in killing any intervention hesitancy within the government.

Frydenberg came up with three options for the fortnightly JobKeeper payment: $1000, $1200 and $1500. They went for the highest number. The package announced on 30 March almost doubled the cost of its predecessor. The "historic wage subsidy" was the only item in the package. It was pitched to help employers keep six million workers, at a cost of $130 billion. What Treasury didn't realise was that it had overestimated the number of workers who would be eligible for the scheme. The final bill was almost a third less than it had budgeted for: $89 billion. When JobKeeper was wound up at the end of March 2021, a total of 3.8 million individuals, counting both workers and sole traders, had received the payment, myself included. The measure of Treasury's relationship with the Morrison government was that there were no recriminations for the counting error.

JobKeeper proved to be the most important piece in the intervention puzzle. It restored confidence after the detail of the two previous packages was swamped by the white noise of lockdown and panic buying.

Okay, it's time to play devil's advocate. I ask Frydenberg to imagine how March 2020 would have played out if Labor had won the 2019 federal election and he was Opposition leader, with Tony Abbott still in the parliament sniping about debt and deficit. He sees where I'm going with the question but doesn't take the bait.

"I'm not into crystal-ball gazing. All I can say is I [never thought] as a Liberal treasurer I'd be producing the largest wage subsidy in Australia's history."

In the end, the Morrison government spent many billions more than was necessary to keep households and businesses afloat during the first twelve months of the pandemic. For lower-income earners in particular, the JobSeeker payment was worth more in their pocket than any part-time work they might have secured before lockdown, while JobKeeper increased the take-home pay of many casual workers. But that was a deliberate policy choice, Josh Frydenberg tells me. It would have been too complicated to include a means test, or a sliding scale of payments for the wage subsidy. The flat amount of $1500 per fortnight was easier to administer. Also, they did not have the luxury of time to design a rort-proof system while hundreds of thousands of people were being laid off.

In March and April 2020, the treasurer's phone was melting down with calls from CEOs pleading for billions of dollars in immediate relief. He drew a line in the sand by saying no to Virgin airlines, to send a message that the government would not be negotiating handouts on a company-by-company basis. JobKeeper gave Frydenberg the leverage to resist these demands because it was unambiguously generous to all firms.

The trade-off was that the safety net was extended to the very top of the income ladder, to businesses and individuals who definitely didn't need support, particularly those who had the luxury of working from home. A small but notable group of publicly listed companies felt guilty enough after reporting healthy profits to pay back some of their JobKeeper. By late March 2021, the Australia Taxation Office had received $160 million from thirty-three firms, including Toyota, which returned its entire $18-million benefit, and the job search agency Seek, which gave back $9.65 million.

Given the gargantuan sums being borrowed and spent on the safety net, no one needed to be worse off. Yet the Morrison government chose to exclude universities from JobKeeper, and also to deny JobSeeker to many of their international students. I asked this question of many people – ministers, former ministers, public servants and vice-chancellors: why were universities singled out? One person familiar with the government's thinking told me: "It's not that complicated. The government hates universities." Another pointed to "the salaries of vice-chancellors."

It is clear the government took the opportunity of the pandemic to force the sector to reduce its dependence on revenue from international students. Frydenberg makes this very point in his explanation for the policy. "There was a sense inside government that universities also had their own financial buffers," he tells me. "They had become very corporatised. They had relied very heavily on international students so they had shifted their business model over time. We were willing to provide very significant support for the universities, but they also had to adjust as other businesses did."

The private schools were also cashed up, but, unlike for the universities, the Morrison government was eager to top up their buffers. Early in the pandemic, the education minister, Dan Tehan, offered to bring forward 25 per cent of annual Commonwealth funding to those independent and Catholic schools prepared to flout state health orders and resume face-to-face teaching. The incentive was aimed at Victoria in particular. Morrison wanted all schools to reopen by June, but the state's premier, Daniel Andrews, would not commit to a timetable while the virus was circulating in the community. Morrison and Andrews were still on good terms at the time, but already testing the boundaries of the federation.

Only forty-six of Victoria's 800 private schools claimed the cash before the premier won the argument for the wrong reason. Victoria's deadly second wave of infections in the winter of 2020 proved that the virus could take off in a school setting and multiply through the population as students infected parents.

The Coalition's preference for private schools over universities had been declared well before the pandemic. It was hiding in plain sight in the budget papers. Universities have been the Commonwealth's sole responsibility since Whitlam's day. But the Commonwealth also has a direct interest in the primary and secondary school systems run by the states for the same reason it has an interest in their health systems: it helps pay the bills for the services they deliver. The governments of Whitlam, Fraser, Hawke and Keating never considered the possibility of giving more money to private schools than universities. Nor did the founder of the modern Liberal Party, Robert Menzies, whose response to the Murray Committee review of the role of universities in Australian life in the 1950s set in train the Commonwealth takeover from the states. "I had a strong feeling that the Commonwealth must be the saviour of the universities, and was glad that in this legislation we had created a precedent," Menzies reflected in his memoir *The Measure of the Years*.

John Howard was the first prime minister to push the Commonwealth in the other direction, to see itself as the saviour of private schools. He explained the mechanics of his approach during interviews for my book *The Longest Decade*. "Prior to us winning office in '96, you couldn't get federal money for a new school in an area that was serviced by a government school and/or a Catholic parish. And it really meant if you wanted to start a school in one of those suburbs that was outside the government or Catholic system, then you couldn't get federal money for it, so we altered that."

The key to the expansion in Commonwealth spending on private schools was Howard's addition of low-fee-paying schools, especially in the outer suburbs, to the federal budget. This background is essential to understanding how the party of Menzies came to exclude the universities from its pandemic safety net.

The final budget of Paul Keating's government in 1995–96 devoted 41.4 per cent of total education spending to higher education. In turn, non-government schools received 16.5 per cent of the total, public schools 10.9 per cent, while a further 4.3 per cent was distributed jointly between them. Labor provided more money directly to students (17.9 per cent of the education budget) than it did to private schools. Eleven years of Coalition government under Howard reversed those priorities. By 2007–08, non-government schools received 35.2 per cent of the total spending, and public schools another 18.2 per cent. The shift came at the expense of higher education, which had its share reduced by almost 9 percentage points, to 32.7 per cent. The precedent would be impossible for subsequent governments to reverse because no party could afford to alienate lower- and middle-income families with children in the private system. The schools, in turn, had an incentive to increase their fees, knowing that government would step in to compensate families. The universities, on the other hand, would be vulnerable to further cuts in the future.

Inevitably, the Coalition came to see education politically, through the eyes of parents. Fee relief for private schools was a perfect wedge issue. Whenever Labor complained about rich schools using taxpayer funds to build new sporting fields, conservative families and swinging voters in outer metropolitan seats thought they would come after their children's education next. But once the children went to university and were old enough to vote, the Coalition wanted some of their money back. The parents might still be Coalition supporters, but their kids were more likely to lean Labor, or even Green. And so the budget was reloaded each year to deliver assistance to the next generation of families who sent their children to private schools at the expense of those who were now studying at university.

Six years of Labor government under Kevin Rudd and Julia Gillard restored higher education to the top line of the budget, although at a significantly lower share to Keating's – 30.3 per cent, compared to 41.1 per cent. Non-government schools had their share reduced from 35.2 per cent to 30 per cent, which was still almost double where it had been under Keating.

The Abbott, Turnbull and Morrison governments went back to a version of the Howard model, driving the share of spending on higher education down to just 24.2 per cent by 2019–20. The universities did the most rational thing in the circumstances. They looked overseas for a new revenue stream. Ordinarily, a conservative government would applaud the initiative and congratulate itself on the market response it had engineered. But if we accept the judgment of my insider source, that success made the Coalition envious.

There were 230,719 overseas students enrolled on Australian campuses in 2013. Six years later, that number had almost doubled, with students from China, India and Nepal driving the growth. This made the universities more reliant on the export side of their business. Overseas students contributed 16 per cent of total university revenue in 2013, and 26 per cent in 2019. This also made higher education our fourth-largest exporter by 2019, behind gas, coal and iron ore, earning almost double that of tourism, which sat in sixth place.

The first pandemic budget guaranteed funding for all domestic university students and provided $1 billion in assistance for research. But the May 2021 budget reverted to type, with no new support. Next year, when the budget assumes the international border will finally reopen, the share of funding for higher education will be at a record low of 23.5 per cent. At that point, even government schools in the state system will receive more money – 24 per cent – while non-government schools will be at an all-time high of 35.7 per cent of the education budget.

Remarkably, spending on higher education is budgeted to fall in absolute terms in the current financial year, and in each of the next two. By 2023–24, spending will be 10.3 per cent lower than when the sector was being short-changed during the pandemic itself. Tribalism still had a seat at the table, even as Morrison absorbed the health and economic briefings from some of the finest public-service minds of his generation.

The Australian National University's vice-chancellor, Nobel laureate Brian Schmidt, appealed to the Coalition's better angels following the budget. He wrote an opinion piece for *The Guardian* explaining how the ANU had anticipated the need for restructure:

> In 2018 ANU made the decision to cap our total student numbers. We sacrificed the revenue growth that would have come through increasing them. In retrospect, this was very unfortunate timing. While we had one of the sector's healthiest balance sheets in 2019, missing a year's growth of student revenue meant the pandemic has hit us harder than anyone in the sector – we have racked up a

> deficit of nearly 15 per cent of our budget in 2020. Sadly, one in 10 of our staff have now departed.
>
> With Australia's borders closed for the foreseeable future, ANU is the canary in the coalmine. The cumulative effect of border closures on international student numbers will lead to other universities catching up with my university's budget woes this year, and worse in the years beyond. This will have a crippling effect on Australia's post-pandemic recovery. Gone will be a large fraction of the $40 billion of export income – the majority of which is not spent in universities, but in the broader Australian economy. Gone will be the large supply of skilled but relatively inexpensive labour. And gone will be the leading-edge research capacity our country needs to prosper post-pandemic, a significant fraction of which is supported by international student fee revenue.

He, like many others in the sector, could not understand why the government had left them to bleed.

Professor Schmidt reminded the government that the success of our COVID response so far was built on "decades of university research."

> There is no shortcut to expertise. We have to constantly grow and nurture it in our universities. New industries and ideas emerge from our campuses and graduates, and the economic spill-overs are large and important.
>
> Of the highly developed nations of the world, Australia is unique in the required level of cross-subsidisation of university research by student fees because the true cost of research is far from covered by the direct funding from research grants. For example, for every dollar of government research grant money a university takes on, it must raise approximately 60 to 70 cents from its students to undertake the research. With the job-ready graduate program pairing domestic student fees to the average cost of delivery, and the collapse of overseas student income, something has

got to give; that will be both the quality and quantity of research, and additional squeezing of what Australian students can expect to get out of their degrees.

This is not a recipe to increase our nation's productivity, nor is it going to allow us to grow Australia in the future through smart immigration.

By denying JobKeeper to the universities in lockdown, the prime minister compromised the sector at a time when the United States and Britain are looking to repair their economies with new investments in education, and recruitment drives for international students.

The very purpose of the safety net was to keep workers attached to their employers and industries, so their jobs would be there when the economy reopened. Without the universities in that net, the education sector, the nation's fifth-largest employer, was almost certain to remain in recession when the others had recovered.

No previous recession was as sudden, nor the recovery as quick. The economy shed 857,000 jobs between February and May 2020, representing 6.6 per cent of the workforce. More than half those jobs (56 per cent) belonged to women, reflecting the disproportionate share of retrenchments borne by the accommodation and food service industry and the arts and recreation services.

Women were the first to be rehired and by March 2021 had returned to their pre-pandemic numbers of employment. Men were one month behind, reaching that benchmark in April. The safety net was vindicated by these headlines.

In a perfect world, every worker would have reclaimed their old job. That did happen for the arts, but not for hotels, restaurants and cafes. The accommodation and food services sectors could only restore 70 per cent of the jobs they had lost to the lockdown. This is not surprising, given the border remained closed to international tourism, and interstate travel carried the risk of a snap lockdown. But elsewhere, the safety net worked as intended. The nation's largest employer, health care and social assistance, recovered all the jobs it had lost, while the second-largest employer, retail, enjoyed a stimulus-led jobs boom and had more people employed by February 2021 than before the pandemic.

The experience of the education sector should have been closer to that of the arts than hospitality. But the denial of JobKeeper meant that it fared even worse than accommodation and food services. Only 60 per cent of the jobs have been recovered, leaving the sector with 35,000 fewer workers in total, or 3.2 per cent of their pre-pandemic workforce. Digging one layer below, the gap is explained almost entirely by the universities, where 30,000 jobs have vanished, representing just under 12 per cent of all academic and staff positions. And as the ANU's vice-chancellor warns, further cuts are inevitable.

Perhaps the better question is not what motivated the rough treatment of higher education in a pandemic, but why the government doesn't fear a community backlash from policy that appears to be based on prejudice, not evidence. The answer can be found in Australia's fractured electorate, and I want to pause to reflect on our political economy before considering the other notable breach in the safety net: aged care.

The Coalition's older, whiter electoral base sees the universities as enemy ground, representing Labor's younger, cosmopolitan base. This makes higher education a soft target for a leader such as Morrison, raised in an era of identity politics.

The fault lines that inform this brand of governing emerged in the aftermath of the 1990s recession, when the Liberal Party became estranged from its cultural roots in Melbourne, the nominal capital of our universities and research institutions. Melbourne's middle-class suburbs represented the nation's political centre behind the tariff wall. They served as an electoral buffer for Menzies throughout the 1950s and '60s. Labor could not form government until it breached the city's mortgage belt in the east and south-east.

Political power flowed through Melbourne in obvious and in subtle ways. The city had been a temporary home of the federal parliament until

1927, creating a habit of aspiration for national leadership. Five of the most significant prime ministers of our first century of federation grew up within a few kilometres of the CBD. Deakin, Bruce and Fraser were born in Melbourne, while Curtin and Menzies hailed from rural Victoria but moved to the city as children.

Bob Hawke, who was born in South Australia and grew up in Western Australia, chose Melbourne as the base from which to build his national profile, first as president of the ACTU in the 1970s and then as the federal member for Wills, in the city's industrial north, from 1980. But it was the Hawke government's pro-market economic reforms which ultimately disenfranchised Melbourne by transferring political power to Sydney, and electoral power to Queensland.

Melbourne was the reason Menzies survived the credit squeeze of 1961. He left the calling of the election as late as possible, to December that year, but he was supremely confident of victory. He had a sixteen-seat majority in a parliament of 122. "There are no circumstances which would suggest even a remote possibility of the Opposition winning seventeen seats," he assured his supporters. The Coalition lost fifteen seats, including eight in Queensland and five in New South Wales. But no seats changed hands in Menzies' home state of Victoria. It was the only time in federal history that the party with a majority of seats in New South Wales and Queensland did not win the election.

The 1990 campaign, held on the eve of the last long recession in Australia, was the mirror image of 1961. Hawke had the luxury of calling an early election in March, just before the recession struck in the second half of the year. Labor had a twelve-seat buffer in a parliament of 148, and it almost disappeared in Victoria alone. Labor lost ten seats there, nine to the Liberals and one through the redistribution of electoral boundaries. One more seat was lost in each of South Australia and Western Australia. If no more seats changed hands, the parliament would have been hung, with Labor on seventy-four, the Coalition seventy-three and one Independent. But Labor picked up two seats from the National

Party in New South Wales and another two from the National Party in Queensland.

It was easy to miss the cultural implications at the time because Australia was operating at two distinct speeds, with Victoria's manufacturing-dependent economy on the brink of recession, while New South Wales and Queensland were still growing. I was part of the press gallery consensus that saw the result through the binoculars of politics and economics. Labor had the superior marginal-seat strategy, and the rugby league states, representing more than half the seats in the federal parliament, were still booming. A status quo election, according to that view. But the bigger story was that Victoria no longer decided who governed Australia.

Almost half the jobs lost in the recession of the early 1990s – 163,000 out of 331,000 – were in Victoria. But its voters were effectively disenfranchised in both the recession and the recovery, as they swung first to the right then to the left while the rest of the nation moved in the opposite direction. The federal Labor government was re-elected in 1993 without a majority of seats in Victoria. Although the state realigned with the nation in 1996, as John Howard's Coalition stormed to power in a landslide, Labor happened to restore its majority in Melbourne at that same election. The significance of the city–country divide was not lost on the new prime minister. The Coalition won more seats in Queensland in 1996 than it did in Victoria. Howard did not need Melbourne to run the country.

Victorians had delivered a majority of seats to the winning party in fourteen out of the eighteen federal elections held between 1946 and 1987. Five of the eight prime ministers in this era represented Victorian electorates: Menzies, Holt, Gorton, Fraser and Hawke.

In the past eleven contests between 1990 and 2019, Victorians were on the winning side just three times, in 1996, 2007 and in the hung parliament of 2010. Queensland, the state which couldn't throw out Menzies in 1961, picked the winner in ten of those eleven elections, with 2010 the sole exception. Five of the last seven prime ministers have been Sydneysiders: Keating, Howard, Abbott, Turnbull and Morrison.

The cultural differences between states mattered less behind the tariff wall, when the parties identified by class, not place. But in a globalised economy, where you live determines how you vote. Australia's political centre moved northwards in the 1990s, as population growth delivered additional seats to Queensland through the redistribution of electoral boundaries. But economic power had been shifting back to Melbourne in the decade between the GFC and the pandemic. The city, and the state, had found a new model of economic growth to replace manufacturing based around skilled migration. Higher education became Victoria's largest export-earner, in a decade when coal was number one in Queensland and New South Wales, and iron ore was the cash cow for Western Australia.

There need not have been a culture war between the two, between the brain economy of the south and the quarry to the north and west. If Howard had honoured the bipartisanship for a clever nation that ran from Menzies to Keating, he could have found a way, for example, to convert some of the windfall from the mining boom into a greater public commitment to higher education. But when he looked at the electoral map, he saw that Melbourne, the birthplace of the Menzies Liberal Party, with its inflated view of itself as the nation's intellectual and moral centre, was expendable. I imagine that Scott Morrison saw the same thing when he decided to leave the universities out of his safety net.

*

Like most Australians, my personal experience of the pandemic was determined by state, not federal, politics. The premier told us when we could leave the house and whom we were allowed to see during lockdown. For Melburnians, that meant just one trip per day to the shops for essential supplies, an hour of exercise within five kilometres of home, no visitors and a curfew between 8 pm and 5 am. Oh, and remember to wear a mask.

The stage four restrictions we faced in the long winter of 2020 physically separated the city from the rest of the state, and Victoria from the rest of the country. The prime minister couldn't fly in, promising relief, while the

Australian people sent us their donations and best wishes. The shared memories of the first lockdown, as the nation moved through the phases of fear then relief, could not be referenced by those outside Melbourne. You had to be here to appreciate the conflicting emotions of dread and stubborn parochial pride that are stirred by a second lockdown. That made us hard to talk to. The best advice to politicians who weren't on the ground was to keep your expressions of sympathy short, and do not, under any circumstances, pass judgment.

Scott Morrison understood that Victorians were annoyed with Daniel Andrews, and we had every right to be. The 800 people who lost their lives to the coronavirus between July and October 2020 exceeded the combined death toll of thirteen years of war in Vietnam, twenty years in Afghanistan and ten years in Iraq. But when the prime minister spoke to Victorians and about Victoria during that second lockdown, he sounded like a carping Opposition leader. In his mind, he was trying to protect us all by forcing Labor to fix its health system and bring it up to the gold standard of New South Wales. And at any other time, he would have been right to shame a recalcitrant state into reform by using the example of a rival. But a pandemic changes the relationship between citizen and government. We want it to succeed, and criticism by outsiders is taken personally.

The politics of lockdown weren't local; they were colonial. This is the defining feature of pandemic life that I think every Australian understood. We had slipped, instinctively, into our pre-federation identities, with Victoria and Queensland separating from Sydney's rule, Western Australia happily closing itself off from the rest of the continent, while South Australia and Tasmania reverted to insularity.

Victoria's difference with New South Wales has always been about the right to set national policy. The two states have reflexively taken opposing positions since the very first federation debate on trade, because the winner gets to define the Australian settlement. In 2020, the health argument was between eliminating and suppressing the virus. Victoria turned the crisis of the second wave into the opportunity of elimination. New South Wales continued to manage the virus with a rigorous regime of testing and tracing everyone who had come into contact with an infected person. But New South Wales and Victoria did have one thing in common: they wanted to keep their borders open with the rest of the country. Queensland shut its border to both from the outset.

While Morrison pressed the states for a consistent border policy, he undermined his own position by singling out the Labor governments in Queensland and Western Australia while avoiding any mention of the Liberal governments that adopted the same uncompromising stance: in South Australia, and especially Tasmania. It took him time to appreciate that most Australians were happy to be separated from one another, if it meant no Victorian-style lockdowns. When the Commonwealth sided with Queensland mining identity Clive Palmer's High Court challenge to Western Australia's hard border in late July 2020, the backlash was so ferocious that the prime minister withdrew from the case within days.

That defeat didn't deter him from picking one last fight with Andrews. By now the second wave was claiming 100 lives a week, with eight out of ten being residents of Commonwealth-run aged-care centres. Morrison wanted all Australians to know that the blame lay with the Victorians. "There are shared responsibilities," he told the ABC's Melbourne-based Michael Rowland on 19 August. "Public health is a matter for the Victorian government, and the federal government regulates aged care." The mild-mannered Rowland replied with the simple fact that aged care is "fundamentally a federal responsibility." The PM would not be deterred: "We regulate aged care, but when there is a public health pandemic, then public health, which, whether it gets into aged care, shopping centres, schools or anywhere else, then they are things that are matters for Victoria."

The journalist in me recorded the pattern. Morrison has never enjoyed scrutiny. The Melburnian in me understood how the victims of the Black Summer fires felt when he told them he didn't hold a hose, mate. The prime minister sounded like a Sydney politician taking a cheap shot.

He must have known how gracelessly he came across because he adopted a more conciliatory tone facing the media later that morning at the AstraZeneca manufacturing plant in North Ryde, in Sydney. The press conference was called to announce that he had "signed a letter of intent with AstraZeneca" to place Australia at the head of the queue to receive the vaccine for COVID-19. "In Victoria and Melbourne at the moment, they're doing it the toughest of all," he said. "My job, the Premier's job today, is just to keep working together to deal with what is in front of us."

The first wave of the virus fractured the federation. The second wave exploited the gaps in the safety net where federal and state powers overlapped, between aged care and the hotel quarantine system for returned travellers. It was a joint failure of governance, and entirely avoidable if the Commonwealth had learnt from the mistakes that were made in aged care during the first wave in New South Wales, and if Victoria hadn't rushed to delegate management of key elements of the hotel quarantine system to the market.

As Peter Rozen, counsel assisting the royal commission into aged care observed, this was the sector the Commonwealth did not have a health plan for: "While there was undoubtedly a great deal done to prepare the Australian health sector more generally for the pandemic, the evidence will reveal that neither the Commonwealth Department of Health nor the aged care regulator developed a COVID-19 plan specifically for the aged care sector."

Although outbreaks in nursing homes were responsible for twenty-eight of the forty-nine deaths in the first wave of the virus in New South Wales, little work was done to prepare the system for the next wave. No target advice was provided by the nation's main COVID advisory body, the Australian Health Protection Policy Committee, in the six critical weeks before the declaration of a state of emergency in Victoria in August. The committee had issued only three statements specific to aged care since February, compared to eight for schools. The implication is that the political push to keep Victoria's private schools open might have distracted the

Commonwealth from its responsibility to keep COVID-19 out of private nursing homes in that state.

The aged-care sector was compromised decades before the virus was carried into its heart by a casualised workforce. The Royal Commission's final report, issued ahead of the 2021 budget, found that no federal government, Coalition or Labor, had ever bothered to ask the threshold question "of how much money is required to offer quality care." The existing system was designed by John Howard's government in 1997 to limit the cost to the budget: a back-to-front mission statement that ensured the market would cut corners. The commission estimated that one in three people in aged care received substandard care, while around one in seven had suffered physical or sexual abuse.

Commissioner Lynelle Briggs found:

> that successive governments have not understood that responsibility for a distributed system like aged care requires hands-on management on the ground. Only Government has the cut-through capability to motivate and direct transformational change of the magnitude we recommend. Not the private sector, not the insurance sector, and not a progressively privatised administration, distant and unaccountable to the community. Only the Government; just as only the Government delivers Medicare and the social security system.

Commonwealth long-term neglect by contracting out fused with Victoria's rushed implementation of hotel quarantine, using private security guards and cleaners without proper training or oversight, to create a perfect viral storm. Victoria's COVID-19 hotel inquiry studied more than 70,000 documents and could not determine who made the decision "to use private security as the first tier of enforcement, or an approval of that rationale in the upper levels of government." But it noted that the Commonwealth had also neglected to inform the states what was expected of them.

> While this Inquiry had no remit or jurisdiction to examine any action or inaction by the Commonwealth, given the role of the Commonwealth through the Commonwealth Pandemic Plan and the lead that it provides to the states and territories, it would be unfair to judge Victoria's lack of planning for a mandatory quarantining program given the Commonwealth, itself, had neither recommended nor developed such a plan.

One observation that brought back memories of the Rudd government's home insulation program was the trust placed in an industry with a vulnerable workforce.

> As an industry, casually employed security guards were particularly vulnerable because of their lack of job security, lack of appropriate training and knowledge in safety and workplace rights, and their susceptibility to an imbalance of power resulting from the need to source and maintain work. These vulnerabilities had previously been identified by the Government. A fully salaried, highly structured workforce with a strong industrial focus on workplace safety, such as Victoria Police, would have been a more appropriate cohort, which would have minimised the risk of outbreaks occurring and made contact tracing an easier job in the wake of an outbreak.

But where the deaths of four young men helped undermine Kevin Rudd's prime ministership in 2010, the deaths of 665 people in the Commonwealth-run aged-care sector in Victoria had no noticeable effect on the electoral position of either Morrison or Andrews in 2020.

Where the GFC triggered an anti-incumbent cycle in Australia, the story of the pandemic so far is that Australians are placing their faith in government again.

Scott Morrison had just six months for clear thinking after his surprise election win in May 2019. The decisions he made in that brief window of unencumbered authority offered a glimpse of his twenty-first-century vision for Australia, before the twin shocks of fire and plague.

He wanted the quiet Australians living outside the cities to know that the government was on their side, defending their blue-collar work and their faith in God. He would begin this project by reorganising the bureaucracy along more masculine lines. He sacked five departmental secretaries, three women and two men, and reduced the total number of Commonwealth departments from eighteen to fourteen. The mergers and demotions, announced on 5 December, sent an unambiguous message to the public service to drop the fancy stuff and focus on job creation. Education was paired with employment, while energy and the environment were broken up, downgrading climate change as a policy concern. The arts were relocated to the blokiest part of the bureaucracy, through the merger of the Department of Communications and the Arts with the Department of Infrastructure, Regional Development and Cities. There wasn't room in the letterhead for all these portfolios, so the arts and cities were left off the new nameplate.

Five days later, he called his last major press conference of the year in Sydney to release new draft legislation promoting religious freedom. He searched for a memorable phrase to assure every Australian that they had nothing to fear from this change. He didn't quite get there: "It is hard to imagine something more personal and in our country, these beliefs and non-beliefs for that matter, are an expression of the liberty to which we all hold dear in countries such as Australia, but especially Australia."

Australia's largest city had been choking in smoke for weeks, and Morrison would have anticipated questions on the fires and their link to climate change. Overnight, his predecessor, Malcolm Turnbull, now a private citizen, had called on the prime minister to coordinate a national response. Morrison replied that he had already announced $11 million in new funding for "aerial firefighting assets" – water bombers. The questions kept coming, and he kept deflecting. Asked if we should be paying volunteer firefighters, he suggested they were happy to work for nothing, and without taking their designated breaks. "In many cases, you've got to hold them back to make sure they get that rest."

The final question returned to Turnbull's observation that "the Coalition is incapable of dealing with climate change because its right wing treats it as an issue of religion or belief, and that is nuts. What's your response to that?" The answer he gave distilled the essence of his prime ministership, then and now. He has an active political brain and a passive policy brain. The latter is only roused when he senses a disturbance in the electoral equation on which he relies for power, in which the Coalition's super-majority in regional Queensland cancels Labor's advantage in the capital cities. "I think Australians take some comfort in the certainty and consistency of our views," he said, signalling he was in no hurry to make climate change a priority. He turned the question on its head, confirming the political calculation that drove him.

> I don't know what the Labor Party thinks anymore, whether it's on climate change or anything else. They seem to be just saying things that people want to hear. They look up their location services enabler and if it says they are in North Queensland, they say one thing, and if they are in Melbourne, they say something else. Australians know they always get the same message from me on this wherever I am in the country, and I think that gives them some certainty. Thank you very much.

The lines he drew that day against intervention disappeared after his return from that ill-advised family holiday to Hawaii. Morrison agreed to pay firefighters on 29 December, and on 6 January announced a $2-billion relief package for victims of the fires, with a promise of more if needed.

The whiplash switch from passive and aggressive to active – the ability to stop thinking politically and start governing – was there before the pandemic. It is the survival instinct of a pragmatist; the most genuinely Australian side of this otherwise unknowable prime minister. Morrison does not appear to have an organised view of the world. This, strangely, is why he was probably the right man to be leading the country in 2020. Only a conservative free of ideology could have dropped the dogma of debt and deficit without prevarication or regret.

In the four decades after Gough Whitlam expanded the size of the national government, the level of Commonwealth expenditure remained largely unchanged, at a long-term average of just under 25 per cent of gross domestic product. Spending was already drifting higher under the Coalition when Morrison had his break-glass moment with the pandemic. In the last financial year, Commonwealth expenditure crossed 32 per cent of GDP and is projected to remain above 26 per cent until the middle of this decade. Net Commonwealth debt will be approaching $1 trillion by then.

Morrison accepted the advice to spend with barely a ripple of dissent within his government, or from those sections of the radio and print media which like to take sides. I doubt that the political system would have been as obliging if Bill Shorten had snuck Labor into power in 2019. The Coalition would have reprised the mantras of Reagan and Thatcher, and Labor might well have tried to split the difference with an intervention too small to prevent a prolonged recession.

But while the health orders and the expanded safety net were critical to the success of Morrison's intervention, they do not answer the pressing questions of the future, starting with the role of government.

Morrison has avoided the question so far because he assumes the old model will reassert itself once the pandemic is over. He has accepted the need to keep spending in the meantime, but refuses to accept greater responsibility for his government.

Big spending alone won't secure quality care for an ageing population. But spending seems to be all the Coalition can think about at the moment. The 2021 budget included $18 billion in new money for aged care over five years, the largest boost to funding for the sector on record. While aged-care royal commissioner Lynelle Briggs welcomed the response to the commission's report, she said, "It's still not enough money to do the job properly." One of the key recommendations that was ignored was to preference direct employment of staff by government over private contractors. The gaps in the safety net which the coronavirus exploited will become poverty traps in recovery if the government continues to defer to the market.

The Commonwealth needs to re-learn the art of running things, or, if it doesn't want the responsibility, to fund the states to take even more matters off its hands. It has effectively given its quarantine powers to the states, albeit without securing a national framework for operation of the system. Perhaps this is the accidental insight for reform in the future: the Commonwealth shifts its gaze as contractor from private-sector providers to the states themselves, with agreements on implementation before any money is spent. The creative democratic tensions in the federation would ensure greater accountability than the present arrangements. Consider, again, the example of aged care. The Commonwealth couldn't answer the simple question of how many frontline workers and residents of nursing homes had been vaccinated because it palmed off the rollout to the private sector without thinking to collect the data, or to enforce compliance if targets weren't met. It did this even though it had promised to vaccinate everyone by Easter; even after the main rollout went off the rails. As of June, fewer than 12 per cent of the sector's 300,000 strong workforce had been fully vaccinated based on estimates by the ABC's Anne Connolly, the investigative journalist whose work led to the original royal commission.

Only the most naive leader would look at the experience of COVID-19 and assume that the next pandemic can be managed with the old model. What the past eighteen months has taught us is that care is primarily the business of government, not the market.

The Commonwealth needs to use the power of its purse to recruit and retain more workers in the caring and brain economies: in early learning, primary, secondary and higher education, in health and aged care, and in disability support. These are all majority female sectors, where wages have been suppressed by government choice. Too often in the past, when crisis created the political opportunity for investment, governments thought with the male side of their brain only and poured billions into infrastructure. It's time to go back to one of the very first reforms Whitlam announced in his first day of power and use the public sector to promote the cause of equal pay for women.

Morrison's approach has posed a question no one thought to ask before the pandemic: who actually runs the country? The answer in this crisis was the National Cabinet, with the premiers claiming their greatest share of power in the federation since Whitlam commenced the long march of centralisation in the 1970s.

The premiers served the national interest well, pushing for a faster lockdown than Morrison wanted. The prime minister adapted, after he realised the new order suited his passive style of governing. He was happy to trade some of the authority of his office for the political gift of appearing blameless.

When the government missed its targets for the vaccine rollout, Morrison called in the states to help while pretending he wasn't in a hurry after all. He shifted the projected date to reopen the international border from the end of 2021 to the middle of 2022, a decision the Treasury says will see around 175,000 people permanently leave Australia during our extended isolation from the rest of the world. The last time we had net emigration outside of war was in the three harshest years of the Great Depression, between 1930 and 1932.

Morrison is tempted by the idea of a little Australia because it offers a simple argument for re-election. The states have already demonstrated the popularity of hard internal borders. Why risk an early return to mass migration when voters are happy with the status quo of zero population growth? Yet one of the practical problems with framing a campaign around border protection is that it handcuffs the Coalition to the old model of contracting out government services. The aged-care sector, for example, will remain compromised while the government can't expand its workforce by recruiting from overseas. The other problem is that it brings forward a reckoning for the universities.

Morrison has no political interest in talking about the future. But passivity does not reduce the threat of another outbreak, or prepare us for the next pandemic. In any case, the future is making demands on Australia in other ways. The new global consensus for intervention would not, of itself, trouble a pragmatist like Morrison. The danger for him is that our allies are taking climate change seriously enough to make an example of Australia.

A decade ago, the Coalition could rely on the obstruction of fellow conservatives in the United States and Canada and the distraction of austerity in the United Kingdom to make the case for inaction. If the world wasn't really interested in climate change, why should we be? Tony Abbott had the good fortune to seize the Liberal leadership on the eve of the climate change conference in Copenhagen in December 2009. Kevin Rudd went to the meeting hoping to be the co-author of a history-making deal. But the talks collapsed, and the Labor prime minister returned home to the taunts of the new Opposition leader.

The experience of the pandemic in the United States and the United Kingdom appears to be having the reverse effect of the global financial crisis; rather than setting back the cause on climate change, it has accelerated momentum for an international agreement to reduce emissions to net zero by 2050. Joe Biden and Boris Johnson have already taken the trouble to snub Morrison at gatherings of world leaders, to send the message that he needs to do better. The US president placed Morrison twenty-second on the list of speakers at his virtual climate summit in April, behind Bhutan, the world's first carbon-negative country, and the recalcitrant Brazil. Curiously, Morrison prepared for that meeting with an attack on climate-change activists. He told a business dinner in Sydney: "We're not going to achieve net zero in the cafes, dinner parties and wine bars of our inner cities."

The British prime minister did not even bother with a B-listing. He simply denied Morrison a speaking slot at the summit he hosted last December. The letter Johnson wrote to Morrison on 8 December 2020, explaining why he had been uninvited, made plain he did not accept the excuse of Coalition disunity. "I welcome your personal commitment to net zero, and I look forward to Australia setting a time bound commitment and an ambitious Nationally Determined Contribution next year [2021]. I recognise how complex these issues are domestically, and your own personal stake in this."

Johnson is hosting the UN climate change summit in Glasgow in November. Will Morrison represent Australia as the passive and aggressive leader, or the pragmatist? He might decide to call an election before then, in the hope he secures a majority large enough to reset Coalition policy. Or he might try to call the bluff of his allies, because he judges it more important to keep his government on the right side of Australia's electoral fault line.

When the US and UK embraced neoliberalism at the end of the 1970s, Australia under Malcolm Fraser paid lip service to that cause without following through. He thought Australians could manage the new global order on our own terms, with the old model of protection that served us since the first decade of federation. He bet the future on a resources boom which never came. It took a recession and a change of government to finally break that model.

Morrison and his ministers are too young to recall this detail, but the Americans imposed their new economic order on the world by changing two key prices. The first was the so-called Nixon shock of 1971, when US president Richard Nixon tore up the old Bretton Woods agreement for fixed exchange rates. Most developed economies responded immediately by floating their currencies. Australia held out for a decade, before the Hawke government floated the dollar in 1983. The second change followed the so-called Volcker shock. The chairman of the US Federal Reserve, Paul Volcker, used punitive interest rates to kill inflation in the United States in the early 1980s. Once again, Australia waited a decade before it followed the American lead. The accumulated cost of inaction could be measured in the recession of the early 1990s, which was deeper and more prolonged than any other in our post-war history.

Global action on climate change looms as the twenty-first-century version of these shocks for Australia. We can pretend that the old model still works just fine for us. But the future will eventually catch up with us.

There is no simple rule for when a government becomes an agent of revolutionary change, but the memory of failure is a crucial element. The Hawke–Keating government, the leaders and their ministers, had lived through the political chaos of the Whitlam era. Before them, Labor's nation-building governments of John Curtin and Ben Chifley and the Coalition government of Robert Menzies had endured two world wars and a depression.

Biden's administration meets this criterion, having governed through the global financial crisis and failed the challenges of recovery. But does Morrison's?

The memory of failure during the 1990s recession, and the lessons of the GFC, informed the advice of Australia's public service during the pandemic. But the challenge of recovery falls on government. The Coalition marks its eighth anniversary in power on 7 September 2021. The first five years were, on its own admission, wasted. The government effectively sacked itself twice, by removing Tony Abbott, then Malcolm Turnbull. The sixth year was devoted to a re-election few expected. Like Abbott, Morrison became prime minister without having had to explain himself properly. He followed the path of least scrutiny to the Lodge because technology and the madness of the past decade of leadership turmoil presented the opportunity. He didn't bend the system to his will; he capitalised on its structural weaknesses.

He had to divide the country to save his government in 2019, pitting the cities against the regions. Those fault lines offer the path of least resistance to re-election now. Doing nothing on climate change, for example, may serve that political interest. But another polarised result can't possibly serve the national interest. Any leader with an interest in Australian history should recognise the warning signs of complacency. Shrinking Australia's ambition to fit an electoral map in which the quarry trumps the brain economy is a model for decline.

Morrison has yet to accept responsibility for the future. The longer he waits, the greater the risk that the rest of the world, led by a reinvigorated United States, imposes its own terms on Australia.

7 June 2021

SOURCES

1 promise to vaccinate Australians by October 2021: Greg Hunt, Doorstop interview about new medications added to the PBS for heart disease and ADHD, 31 January 2021; Inga Ting, Nathanael Scott and Alex Palmer, "Untangling Australia's vaccine rollout timetable", ABC News online, 28 May 2021, updated 30 May 2021; "Australia's COVID-19 vaccine national rollout strategy", Presentation, Australian Government, www.health.gov.au/sites/default/files/documents/2021/01/covid-19-vaccination-australia-s-covid-19-vaccine-national-roll-out-strategy.pdf.

2 "The Government": Scott Morrison, "Each day we are now updating information on the roll out of the vaccine" [Facebook status], 11 April 2021, accessed 31 May 2021.

2 Australians would be at the head of the global queue for vaccines: Scott Morrison, Media release, 19 August 2020.

2 admission that the exercise had run off the rails: Scott Morrison, Doorstop – Castle Hill, New South Wales, 14 March 2021.

JOURNALIST: On the graph, Prime Minister, it looked like not all of the first doses will be administered by October?

PROFESSOR BRENDAN MURPHY, SECRETARY OF THE DEPARTMENT OF HEALTH: Well, that's not true.

PRIME MINISTER: That's not true. It actually says that all are done by the end of October. That's what the graph actually shows.

2 "Don't go to Facebook": Scott Morrison, Q&A, National Press Club, Barton, ACT, 1 February 2021.

2 the plan was foiled: Lenore Taylor, "ETS off the agenda until late next term", *The Sydney Morning Herald*, 27 April 2010.

3 "Given that": Kevin Rudd, Doorstop, Nepean Hospital, Penrith, 27 April 2010.

3 "Now, I've been asked": Scott Morrison, Statement – Update on COVID-19 Vaccination Program, 12 April 2021.

That second Facebook statement, which was reproduced on his official site, was more disingenuous than the first because it pretended that Morrison had never been in the business of setting targets. In fact, the October deadline – the original two jabs program, and the revised single-jab program – had been developed with one eye on the political calendar. The prime minister wanted the option of calling an election later in 2021 to coincide with the completion of the vaccine rollout.

3 "lost the support": Mark Butler, *Climate Wars*, extracted in *The Guardian*, 5 July 2017.

3 Public satisfaction with democracy: Australian National University, "Trust in government hits all-time low", ANU website, 9 December 2019, www.anu.edu.au/news/all-news/trust-in-government-hits-all-time-low, accessed 1 June 2019.

5 third-lowest death rate: On the first anniversary of Australia's move into lockdown, 13 March 2021, the total number of lives lost to COVID-19 was 909, or 35 per million people. If Australia suffered the death rates of the US or Italy, we would have lost around 43,000 lives. The UK death rate, the worst in the G20, would have pushed out the death toll to almost 48,000. The differences remain stark if you measure our performance against more competent rich countries in the middle of the table – namely, Canada and Germany. Canada's death rate translated to more than 15,000 Australia lives lost, while Germany's was almost 23,000. (My calculations are based on the UK's 1840 per million, Italy's 1682 per million, the United States' 1641 per million, Germany's 879 per million and Canada's 590 per million.)

The UK had delivered at least one dose of COVID-19 vaccine to 35.6 per cent of its population by 13 March, while the United States was ranked second with 20.6 per cent. Australia's vaccination rate at the time was just 0.6 per cent, the worst in the G20, based on the Our World in Data tables. The UK crossed the 50 per cent threshold on 27 April, while the US was at 42.4 per cent. Unfortunately, we don't have a direct comparison for Australia for this date, so I've taken the health department's total vaccine doses of 2,029,544 as at 27 April and divided by the total population of 25.78 million. The actual figure will be much lower than 7.9 per cent implied here as some people will have received two doses.

www.worldometers.info/coronavirus/?fbclid=IwAR3FPvmohbyPDK4iTU7ZqfLtXaf5nXK42lX5nXE14nRWos1AB4-W-Eh9LQQ

https://ourworldindata.org/covid-vaccinations

https://www.health.gov.au/sites/default/files/documents/2021/04/covid-19-vaccine-rollout-update-28-april-2021.pdf

www.abs.gov.au/ausstats/abs%40.nsf/94713ad445ff1425ca25682000192af2/1647509ef7e25faaca2568a900154b63?OpenDocument

5 Australia was at the bottom of the table: *Financial Times* figures at 2 June 2021. At the time of writing, Victoria was in the second week of a lockdown and demand for vaccinations in the state was surging after weeks of complacency.

7 $2.3-trillion infrastructure program: The White House, "Fact sheet: The American families plan", 28 April 2021. *The New York Times* has a handy breakdown of the infrastructure and family packages: www.nytimes.com/2021/04/28/upshot/biden-families-plan-american-rescue-infrastructure.html.

9 "Any way you slice it": Nathaniel Rakich, "Biden's betting on public support to push his agenda: Polls show his big spending packages have it", *FiveThirtyEight*, 30 April 2021.

9 Almost one in four US citizens (24 per cent) were out of work: The unemployment rate remained above 10 per cent until 1941, on the eve of America's entry into World War II (see https://fred.stlouisfed.org/graph/?g=jS03). Roosevelt was lucky that the second wave of the Depression struck in May 1937, six months after his re-election, and had ended well before the 1940 campaign. See: www.nber.org/research/data/us-business-cycle-expansions-and-contractions.

11 federal deficit: My calculations using the total budget measure from Table 1.2 – "Summary of receipts, outlays, and surpluses or deficits (–) as percentages of GDP: 1930–2025, www.whitehouse.gov/omb/historical-tables.

11 "These findings": David Hope and Julian Limberg, "Footing the COVID-19 bill: Economic case for tax hike on wealthy", *The Conversation*, 17 December 2020; David Hope and Julian Limberg, "The economic consequences of major tax cuts for the rich", Working Paper 55, International Inequalities Institute, London School of Economics, December 2020.

12 "It was too punitive": Robert Reich, "Bidenomics beats Reaganomics and I should know – I saw Clintonomics fail", *The Guardian*, 14 March 2021.

12–13 "Ten minutes of talkback": Don Watson, *Recollections of a Bleeding Heart*, Knopf, 2002, p. 667.

13–14 "As a senator": Reich, "Bidenomics".

14 deepest recession since the Great Depression: The NBER plots the start of the recession in January 2008 and its conclusion in June 2009. The unemployment rate was 7.8 per cent in January 2009, and peaked at 10 per cent in October.

15 "It has to be": Deaton quoted in Roge Karma, "'Deaths of despair': The deadly epidemic that predated the coronavirus", *Vox*, 15 April 2020.

15 "You know, the confidence": Remarks by President Biden at the House Democratic Caucus Virtual Issues Conference, 3 March 2021.

15 "We're not going to make the mistake of 2008 and 2009": Chuck Schumer, *Anderson Cooper 360 Degrees*, CNN, 9 March 2021.

16 "The age of irresponsibility": David Cameron, "The age of austerity", Speech, 26 April 2009.

16 The European Union … slipped into a double recession: Quarterly GDP Total, Percentage change, previous period, Q2 1947 – Q4 2020 Source: Quarterly National Accounts, https://data.oecd.org. The GFC recession ended for the EU as a whole in the September quarter of 2009, after five conservative quarters of so-called "negative" growth. The double-dip recession commenced in the December quarter of 2011 and ran for six quarters until growth resumed in the June quarter of 2013.

17 "go back to what people called austerity": Lizzy Buchan, "Boris Johnson says coronavirus has been 'disaster' for UK and suggests 'Rooseveltian' approach to rebuilding economy", *The Independent*, 29 June 2020.

20 first iteration: The pattern of political hesitancy and bureaucratic overkill had been established in the very first crisis of the Menzies era, the Korean War wool boom and bust. Wool prices had already peaked, and began tumbling five months before Arthur Fadden delivered his infamous "horror budget" in September 1951. Writing in the official history of the Reserve Bank from 1945 to 1975, Professor Boris Schedvin said it was "difficult to explain why so little note was taken of the collapse in the price of wool." He suggested that the goal was to maintain control over the politicians. "As the [Menzies] government had been so difficult to persuade, senior officials were unwilling to encourage backsliding by softening their recommendations in the light of altered circumstances." Treasury, "Arthur Fadden, treasurer in a golden age", Treasury website, 30 March 2012.

21 "Shut up": Obituaries Australia, https://oa.anu.edu.au/obituary/wheeler-sir-frederick-henry-1567.

22 "begun too late; it was too severe; it lasted too long.": See Treasury biography of Frank Crean, https://treasury.gov.au/publication/economic-roundup-issue-2-2013-2/economic-roundup-issue-2-2013/frank-crean-a-long-wait-for-a-turbulent-tenure.

28 next election campaign: As a victim and then a beneficiary of this process, Howard had the good sense to end it. A charter of budget honesty was introduced after the 1996 election to ensure no more surprises. It required Treasury to produce an independent update of the budget numbers at the start of each campaign.

28 Rudd's catch-cry: In truth, there had not been that much difference between Kevin Rudd and John Howard in the 2007 campaign. Kevin Rudd matched every generous tax cut and handout the government announced but shaved off a billion dollars here and there so he could claim the larger surplus. The centrepiece of Howard's re-election bid were personal tax cuts valued at $34 billion over three years. Rudd matched 90 per cent of that amount – $31 billion – and used $2.3 billion of the $3 billion left over to fund a family tax break for education expenses, to be paid over two years. Howard then promised his own education tax refund worth $6.3 billion over four years.

28 construction sector: The construction sector employed 991,500 workers on the eve of the GFC, in August 2008. At the peak of the infrastructure cycle in August

2011, the figure was 1.021 million, reflecting both the school buildings program and the windfall to our economy from China's own stimulus program. A year later, after more than 60,000 workers had been laid off, the construction sector was back to where it started, with 981,900 people employed.

28 The chair of the royal commission: Ian Hanger wrote: "The reality is that the Australian Government conceived of, devised, designed and implemented a program that enabled very large numbers of inexperienced workers – often engaged by unscrupulous and avaricious employers or head contractors, who were themselves inexperienced in insulation installation – to undertake potentially dangerous work. It should have done more to protect them." Ian Hanger, *Report of the Royal Commission into the Home Insulation Program*, Commonwealth of Australia, 2014.

34 "The age of entitlement is over": Joe Hockey, Budget speech 2014–15, 13 May 2014.

35 "a government that says what it means": Tony Abbott, Acceptance speech, 7 September 2013.

37 Treasury wasn't forecasting a bushfire recession: On the three previous occasions that the nation's output of goods and services had fallen in a single quarter – because of the Queensland floods in the March quarter of 2011, the global financial crisis in the December quarter of 2008, and a mini housing crash in the December quarter of 2000 – the economy rebounded by at least 1 per cent in the next quarter. Australian Bureau of Statistics, *Australian National Accounts National Income, Expenditure and Product*, 3 December 2020, www.abs.gov.au/statistics/economy/national-accounts/australian-national-accounts-national-income-expenditure-and-product/latest-release, accessed 1 June 2021.

In the end, the economy contracted by a modest 0.4 per cent in the March quarter, and by a record 7 per cent in the lockdown June quarter. The next two quarters saw growth of 3.4 per cent and 3.1 per cent respectively, leaving the economy 1.1 per cent smaller at the end of 2020 than it had been a year earlier.

38 "Much of Australia's future": Frydenberg in *Hansard*, 25 October 2010.

39 wages growth had fallen to record lows: Australian Bureau of Statistics, "Wage price index, Australia", March 2021, released 19 May 2021, www.abs.gov.au/statistics/economy/price-indexes-and-inflation/wage-price-index-australia/latest-release, accessed 1 June 2021.

39 government expenditure crept to an even higher level: Average spending as a share of GDP for Labor over the five years from the GFC in 2008–09 to their final budget in 2013–15 was 24.9 per cent. The Coalition's average from 2014–15 to 2019–20, the last budget before the pandemic, was 25 per cent (my calculations from the budget papers).

40 "and well below market expectations": Alyssa Leng and Roland Rajah, "Chart of the week: Global trade through US–China lens", Lowy Institute website, 18 December 2019, www.lowyinstitute.org/the-interpreter/chart-week-global-trade-through-us-china-lens, accessed 1 June 2021.

42 our debt was low by international standards: 2018–19 gross debt comparisons are from Annex Table 1. General Government Fiscal Balance and Gross Debt, 2018–21: Overall Balance and Gross Debt, International Monetary Fund, *World Economic Outlook, Update June* 2020, www.imf.org/en/Publications/WEO/Issues/2020/06/24/WEOUpdateJune2020. Net debt figure is from Table 11.4: Australian government general government sector net debt and net interest payments, from the budget papers.

43 business was at the front of the queue: Payments to boost business cash flow carried a price tag of $6.7 billion, another $3.2 billion was spent on incentives for business to invest, and $1.3 billion in wage subsidies was provided to small firms. The $750 payment to pensioners and others on income support totalled $4.9 billion. Rudd's first stimulus was valued at $10.4 billion at the time, or $13.2 billion in 2020 dollars, after adjusting for inflation.

43 "It was very apparent": Steven Kennedy, Senate committee hearing, 28 April 2020.

44 "The Board will not increase": Reserve Bank of Australia, Statement of Philip Lowe, governor: Monetary policy decision, media release, 19 March 2020.

45 number of people receiving the supersized dole: My calculations from Department of Social Security dataset Table 1: Recipients of Newstart Allowance, JobSeeker Payment, Bereavement Allowance, Sickness Allowance and Youth Allowance – Time Series.

48 "Scott Morrison managed": Simon Benson, "Premiers lost their nerve, they should be ashamed", *The Australian*, 23 March 2020.

48 "All sides are now claiming": David Crowe, Rob Harris and Alexandra Smith, "How the shutdown talk ahead of national cabinet spread confusion", *The Age* and *The Sydney Morning Herald*, 23 March 2020.

50 "chalk and cheese": David Gruen to Sabra Lane, *AM*, ABC Radio, 20 August 2020.

50 3.8 million individuals: See box 2.4, page 60 of Budget Statement No. 1, https://budget.gov.au/2021-22/content/bp1/download/bp1_2021-22.pdf

51 $160 million from thirty-three firms: Matthew Elmas, "Only five profitable companies have repaid their JobKeeper windfalls", *The New Daily*, 26 March 2021.

52 Only forty-six of Victoria's 800 private schools claimed the cash: Paul Karp, "Coalition offers independent schools early funding if they return to face to face teaching", *The Guardian*, 29 April 2020; Anna Prytz, "Independent schools snub early funding lure to reopen classrooms", *The Age*, 7 May 2020.

53 "I had a strong feeling": Robert Menzies, *The Measure of the Years*, Cassell, 1970, p. 83.

53 "Prior to us winning office": George Megalogenis, *The Longest Decade*, Scribe, 2008 revised and updated edition, pp. 199–200.

55 Overseas students: Hazel Ferguson and Susan Love, "The impact of COVID-19 on Australian higher education and overseas students – what do the numbers say?", Parliament of Australia website, posted 12 August 2020, www.aph.gov.au/About_Parliament/Parliamentary_Departments/Parliamentary_Library/FlagPost/2020/August/Universities_and_COVID, accessed 1 June 2021.

55 By 2023–24, spending will be 10.3 per cent lower: See table 6.7 from the budget papers.

The deficits over this period are $83.5 billion, or 4.3 per cent of GDP; $161 billion (7.8 per cent of GDP); $106.6 billion (5 per cent of GDP); $99.3 billion (4.6 per cent) and $79.5 billion (3.5 per cent).

55 "In 2018 ANU made the decision", etc.: Brian Schmidt, "Universities have been left to bleed in the budget but we are pivotal to the recovery", *The Guardian*, 12 May 2021.

57 In a perfect world: The industry employment figures compare February 2020 with February 2021.

59 sixteen-seat majority: The ACT and Northern Territory elected a member each to the parliament, bringing the total number of seats to 124, but they did not have voting rights on the floor.

59 "There are no circumstances": David Lee, "Issues that swung elections: The 'credit squeeze' that nearly swept Menzies from power in 1961", *The Conversation*, 30 April 2019.

61 Higher education became Victoria's largest export-earner: Department of Foreign Affairs and Trade, "Australia's Trade by State and Territory, 2018–19", Statistics Section, Trade & Investment Economics Branch, Office of the Chief Economist, Australian Government, Canberra, May 2020, www.dfat.gov.au/sites/default/files/australia-state-territory-2018-19.pdf.

62 The 800 people: Coronavirus death toll taken from www.dhhs.vic.gov.au/victorian-coronavirus-covid-19-data; war casualty figures from www.awm.gov.au/articles/encyclopedia/war_casualties.

63 "We regulate": Scott Morrison, Interview with Michael Rowland, *ABC News Breakfast*, 19 August 2020.

64 "signed a letter of intent": Scott Morrison, Press conference, Macquarie Park, NSW, 19 August 2020.

64 twenty-eight of the forty-nine deaths: Figures as at 1 July 2020, when the national death was 104; www.health.gov.au/resources/collections/coronavirus-covid-19-at-a-glance-infographic-collection#july-2020.

65 "of how much money", and "that successive governments": Royal Commission into Aged Care Quality and Safety, *Final Report*, 1 March 2021.

65–6 "to use private security", "While this inquiry" and "As an industry": COVID-19 Hotel Quarantine Inquiry, *Final Report*, 21 December 2020.

68 "I think Australians take some comfort": Scott Morrison, Press conference, Sydney, New South Wales, 10 December 2019.

69 Commonwealth expenditure crossed 32 per cent of GDP: The average from the Hayden budget 1975–76 to the aftermath of the final budget of the Rudd–Gillard era in 2013–14 was 24.8 per cent (my calculations from the budget papers).

70 "It's still not enough money": Sandy Cheu, "Budget measures insufficient to fix aged care: Briggs", Australian Ageing Agenda, 20 May 2021.

70 estimates by the ABC's Anne Connolly: Anne Connolly, "Aged care COVID vaccination blame game hits a new low – and residents are collateral damage", ABC News (online), 2 June 2021.

72 "We're not going to achieve": Scott Morrison, Address, Business Council of Australia Annual Dinner, Sydney, New South Wales, 19 April 2021.

Correspondence

Tim Flannery

Dr Alan Finkel was Australia's eighth chief scientist, serving from January 2016 until he was succeeded by Dr Cathy Foley in 2021. Finkel describes himself as an engineer (the field in which he trained), and he has held many illustrious positions, including president of the Australian Academy of Technology and Engineering. The approach Finkel takes in *Getting to Zero* stems from his engineering background. Notably, it builds on a speech he gave to the National Press Club on 12 February 2020 and indeed recycles much of his Press Club text verbatim.

At the time Finkel addressed the National Press Club, he was speaking as Australia's chief scientist and representing Australian science. Yet his words so concerned twenty-five of Australia's top climate scientists that they penned a letter in response. While welcoming Finkel's role in helping to expand renewable energy, the scientists expressed concern "about the scale and speed of the decarbonisation challenge required to meet the Paris Agreement and, in particular, [Finkel's] support for the use of gas as a transition fuel over 'many decades.'" They concluded that Finkel's approach was inconsistent with a safe climate, and they found no evidence that Australia needs an expanded gas industry in order to transition to renewables.

How could the chief scientist give a major address so out of kilter with the country's most eminent scientists? The answer, I think, can be read between the lines in *Getting to Zero*, which is essentially an assessment of the technologies required to achieve deep emissions cuts in the eight sectors of the Australian economy that produce greenhouse gases.

The first and largest of these sectors is electricity generation, and Finkel does a great job outlining the scale of the transition required for it to reach net zero. To convert Australia's electricity supply to solar and wind, he says, we would need to increase the current electricity production from wind and solar sevenfold. But if we hope to electrify the entire economy (including transport and industry), we'd need to do that three times over and to store energy on an unprecedented scale at the same time. Finkel's analysis here is masterly, and his analysis would meet with agreement from the nation's scientists.

But it's the role of gas in achieving net zero that is contested. Energy minister Angus Taylor has called for a gas-led economic recovery, and in the past Finkel has echoed the minister's view that we need more gas. In *Getting to Zero*, Finkel soft-pedals on the issue, saying only that "it is not clear at this time whether existing gas generators will be sufficient to provide firming services." Notably, he also backs away from his previous openness to nuclear power, saying that the cost of electricity from conventional nuclear is "too high," while leaving the door open to smaller nuclear reactors that are not yet developed.

In his Press Club address, Finkel talked up the virtue of making hydrogen from coal and gas, arguing that carbon capture and storage (CCS) can be economical in sequestering the carbon dioxide generated in the process. In *Getting to Zero*, he says, "The main criticism directed at producing hydrogen from fossil fuels is that it will proceed without carbon capture and storage. Wrong." Yet this is exactly what is happening right now at Australia's first coal-to-hydrogen plant (in Victoria's La Trobe Valley). While the plant claims to be "carbon capture–ready," right now it's venting carbon dioxide into the atmosphere at the rate of around 88 kilograms for every kilogram of hydrogen created. If CCS is as economical as Finkel suggests, why isn't it being used by the industry from the outset?

Finkel also outlines an interesting synergy between hydrogen and gas, pointing out that generators running on gas can easily be converted to hydrogen, as can many pipelines. The effect of this claim is to blunt opposition to new gas infrastructure. In light of Finkel's claim regarding fossil fuels, CCS and hydrogen, I'm sceptical that the conversion to hydrogen will occur in a timely manner.

Finkel's detailed assessment of what remains to be done to reach net-zero emissions makes it clear that the nation faces an immense task. On this all agree. The real question is how quickly it must be done, and on this point Finkel is largely silent, focusing instead on how long it would take given current economic and technological constraints. The thing climate scientists know, but which Finkel does not fully acknowledge, is that the time we have to achieve the task will be determined by the Earth's system. If we trigger one or more of Earth's nine climate tipping points, we may find ourselves irrevocably sliding towards catastrophic climate change. If that happens, nothing we do with our energy systems will alter our fate. So the key question becomes: how quickly do we need to decarbonise our economy to give us a fair chance (a 66 per cent chance, say) of avoiding catastrophic change? Scientists are currently working on an answer, and their early findings suggest that by 2050 it will be too late.

As with all transitions, the closer a deadline looms, the more expensive it is to achieve: long before it becomes impossible, it becomes extremely costly. For argument's sake, let's examine the implications of needing to reach net zero by 2035. Australia would need to close all of its coal in the next eight and a half years and build seven times more wind- and solar-powered energy systems than we've built to date. But that would only be the start. Australia would need to repeat the exercise more than twice over to electrify transport and industrial energy completely. We'd need to retire hundreds of billions of dollars' worth of assets, including steel mills, aluminium plants, coalmines and power plants, and of course almost every vehicle in the country. Given the technological obstacles, and the lack of incentive in our current economic model, this would not be achievable in the Australia of today. The only way to reach net zero would be to put the nation on a war footing, as Australia did in 1939 (and again in 2020 when confronted by the COVID-19 pandemic). When a nation is in a struggle for its very existence, nobody counts the cost. The imperative is to win regardless.

Finkel refuses to countenance this possibility, saying that "it is simply unrealistic to think that with political will we can immediately reverse course." He adds: "No trade-off, no dichotomy. Prosperity *and* low emissions. It is my firm belief we can have both." Before the year is out, scientists are likely to publish their analysis on when we need to reach net-zero emissions. I would be interested in speaking to Finkel at this point, to see what he makes of it.

Finkel uses several ruses to respond to those who want action commensurate with the scale and immediacy of the threat. For example, he puts up the straw man that we cannot immediately shut down coal. And, although he is no longer chief scientist, he steers clear of discussing the role of government and the impacts of policy. Finkel is a good engineer, saying that "the first step in developing a solution is to identify the problem." Yet in *Getting to Zero*, he tragically fails to do that: the real problem, as climate scientists know, is that unless we take timely action and view cost as a secondary consideration, we seem destined to precipitate a new, dangerous climate that will threaten our global civilisation.

Tim Flannery

GETTING TO ZERO

Correspondence

Scott Ludlam

Alan Finkel's forceful review of what "getting to zero" could actually look like is at once bracing, daunting and cautionary.

It is bracing because it is confirmation – from someone who should know – that there are no significant engineering barriers to a near-zero carbon economy. As chief scientist, Dr Finkel has worked at the highest level for successive governments; he has an unusual combination of scientific credentials and political survival skills, earned in the toxic swamp of national energy debates.

In the 1990s and early 2000s, it was left largely to civil society organisations such as Greenpeace and Beyond Zero Emissions to make the case that we could ramp down fossil combustion while keeping the lights on. That was important work: it moved the debate forward and gave confidence to the non-technical among us that we weren't asking the impossible. But it meant pushing against the heavy headwinds of the establishment, with the terms of debate set by industry incumbents. Even if such a transition were necessary, they insisted it could only be done with nuclear power, 'clean' coal or some *Star Trek* invention that didn't exist yet.

It's worth pausing to appreciate just how far we've come. The way is clear for a zero-emissions electricity grid powered by the sun and wind, and distributed backup in the form of batteries and pumped hydro. Sector by sector, the future is here; now it's just a question of scaling it up. As for the sacred cows of coal and gas exports, Dr Finkel takes direct aim at them, illuminating the writing on the wall in capital letters ten feet high: it's over. We can build export industries of hydrogen, green steel and direct electricity supplies to our neighbours, or we can watch coal, gas and uranium revenues collapse as the rest of the world moves ahead without us. These are political questions we're grappling with, not technical ones. For those who've spent years – or decades – at this coalface, this is an affirmation, from the heart of the establishment, that we've been on the right track all along.

Dr Finkel's essay is daunting as well, because it doesn't shy away from just how much work we have left to do, the scale of the proposed build and the consequences of further delay. It's useful to fill in some of the blanks here: the reason we're so late to this isn't the fault of technologists or people working in the clean-energy sector. It's because energy multinationals and their allied media platforms have thoroughly poisoned our politics over the course of three decades. The peak bodies for mining, oil and gas spent millions brutally dispatching the Rudd and Gillard governments, and installing the greasily compliant Abbott and Morrison, with a pause along the way to cancel the Turnbull experiment. Those powerful lobbyists won't back down just because the former chief scientist declares them obsolete; their grip on state and federal politics now approaches a level that in other countries would be considered a form of state capture.

This is a fight that won't be resolved through reasoned argument alone: if that were possible, those reports by Greenpeace and Beyond Zero would have concluded the debate years ago. Instead, we're forced to conduct it in the teeth of megafires and rising seas. For Dr Finkel's blueprint to take physical form in the time we may have left, it will take a full-scale rebellion, encompassing everything from shareholder activism and electoral upsets to mass-occupations of corporate headquarters and mine sites.

That's where the cautionary aspect of the essay comes into sharpest relief. As an engineer, Dr Finkel is tasked with optimising a technology mix to drive emissions down as rapidly as possible. He covers a huge amount of ground in a short space – from power stations to private cars, agriculture to aluminium smelters – so it's not a criticism to note that wider social and historical imperatives are beyond the essay's scope. But some of this context matters. Finkel proposes replacing fossil generators and exporters with renewable ones, while leaving the rest of society much as it is. Over a thirty-year build, it is estimated that a high-end solar field would occupy an astonishing 20,000 square kilometres of land. Clearly this is not on the same scale of apocalyptic destruction as longwall coal-mining or gas fracking, but on whose land will these new clean energy projects be built? Where will the rare earths come from? Will access agreements be imposed on traditional owners, using the unforgivably coercive framework of native title, or will we at last discuss sovereignty and land rights?

It's also worth reflecting on the conclusion reached by the International Energy Agency in 2018 that 40 per cent of the world's energy use could be eliminated through humble efficiency retrofits and improvements to building and product designs. Finkel only glances at this potential; while such measures are less glamorous than a new offshore wind farm, that's an astonishing amount of electricity we can choose not to use at all. Rather than relying on brute-force generation to power everything from seawater desalination to air conditioning in poorly designed building stock, we could shift our focus to low-impact design.

A similarly unglamorous approach to transport is needed. There's every reason to be excited about the proliferation of electric cars heralding the long-delayed extinction of the internal combustion engine. But there's not enough lithium – or car parking – for everyone to own a two-tonne electric SUV, even if we wanted to deploy enough photovoltaic solar energy to power them. Older disciplines of public transport, compact, transit-oriented urban design and truly accessible cities can help to inform our decisions if we broaden our horizons beyond trying to replace coal and gas with the equivalent installation of solar and wind.

None of this is to say I disagree with the essay's basic premise: the renewable future is here if we're ready to seize it. But in accepting this premise, a whole range of options and possible futures opens up. One option is to try to maintain our energy-profligate, infinite-growth society through a massive deployment of solar, wind and storage. Another option is to choose a path of lower impact; to embed the energy agenda within the wider ambition of land rights, regenerative economics and circular design principles. With our current government so manifestly unfit to even initiate this conversation, it's up to the rest of us to make it happen. Then the engineers and the technologists can really get to work.

Scott Ludlam

GETTING TO ZERO

Correspondence

Ross Garnaut

Alan Finkel has his critics on climate change in the scientific and policy communities. They argue that his prescriptions would do too little, too late, and provide cover for vested interests influencing policy to continue in old ways.

This response provides another context for Alan's work on climate change as chief scientist from 2015 to 2020 and now as our prime minister's special adviser on climate and the energy transition. The latter role is of national significance, through the series of demanding heads-of-government conferences in which Scott Morrison participates as a member or observer. The meetings commenced with President Biden's virtual Climate Summit in April 2021, and will continue through the G7 in London and the G20 in Rome, to the Glasgow conference of the parties to the UN Framework Convention on Climate Change hosted by UK prime minister Boris Johnson in December.

We should be under no illusion about what is at risk through these international meetings: Australia's reputation as a nation that pulls its weight as a member of the international community of democratic countries. We should be under no illusion that our national interest is at risk, as the country which stands to lose most from failure on global climate change mitigation and to gain most economically from full participation in success.

Australians who understand what is at stake can be glad that Alan Finkel has the ear of senior figures in a government that in its early years had resisted scientific reality and set out to remove effective instruments for reducing Australian emissions. In *Superpower: Australia's Low-Carbon Opportunity*, I said that the prospects of building Australia's prosperity by embracing the world's movement to zero net emissions is the bridge over which the Morrison government can walk across the chasm, from the spoiling side of climate action to constructive participation. Alan points out to government that stepping onto this bridge is necessary and safe.

But we have to make sure that the bridge, which has scientific, engineering and economic components, goes all the way to the other side. In *Getting to Zero*, Alan describes himself as an engineer. The engineering design is in good hands. We must make sure the scientific and economic components are soundly built as well.

The engineering

Getting to Zero presents a fascinating description of how the chief scientist and Australian governments became committed to major use of hydrogen in the transition. Alan calls hydrogen the hero of the story and describes its many potential roles. He expects it to play a big role in the future Australian economy. He is probably right, in a time frame that will allow him to see the fruits of his work.

Getting to Zero provides background on the development of the 2020 First Low Emissions Technology Statement – or Roadmap. It says a little about the selection of five technologies that will have higher priority than others for government support: clean hydrogen; energy storage; carbon capture and storage in geological structures; low-emissions steel and aluminium; and soil carbon. In the absence of a carbon price, government fiscal support is the main policy instrument for promoting the application of new technologies. Priorities guide government allocation decisions. All technologies on the list will have a role in a future zero-emissions economy. Others have strong claims. I hope that they are not neglected. Alan says that they can be added later.

Alan tells an interesting story of his involvement in the review of Australian energy institutions after the blackout in South Australia in 2016. Political partisans blamed the blackout on the high proportion of renewable energy. Alan explains that the problem was the National Electricity Market's operation and design, and not an excess of renewables. As the system operators have gained experience, "it is now clear that it will be possible to achieve the ultimate goal of a zero-emissions electricity system." Alan has contributed to that learning from experience.

The science

Getting to Zero describes the scientific basis of climate change and the need for climate action in a simple and compelling way. Alan and I, engineer and economist, both absorb the realities of atmospheric physics from specialists in the field. Alan presents the scientific reality faithfully: theory tells us that increased carbon dioxide and methane, and to a lesser extent other greenhouse gases, raise the average temperature and reduce variations in the temperature of the atmosphere, and also of the land and sea; human activity over the past century or so has already lifted average global temperatures by around 1.2 degrees (1.4 degrees on average in Australia); increasing concentrations of greenhouse gases destabilise the climate upon which established patterns of life on Earth depend; damage has already been done, and increases with each increment of emissions. We have to get to net zero by about the middle of the century. There is no reasonable cause for doubt; denial is irrational. We can be glad that our federal leaders have been exposed to such clear expression of important truth.

Alan ends his discussion of the science by saying that "zero" really means low or very low; that low really means less than 10 per cent from where we started. My reading of the physics raises questions about that reinterpretation of zero. Ten per cent of where Australia started, or where the world started? Ten per cent of Australia in 2005 is an amount per person that is around half of where the world was in 2005, or about the whole of where India was. Would India think it reasonable to stay at Australia's 10 per cent, or the world's? Which of these would be fair? Which of these would be acceptable?

Be that as it may, my reading of the physics says that concentrations of greenhouse gases in the atmosphere and the trend in global temperatures will continue to rise while net emissions exceed zero. Absolute zero, not 10 per cent of an old number. The Summary for Policy Makers in the IPCC's Special Report on Global Warming of 1.5°C says that to hold temperature increases to 1.5 degrees, we have to have net-zero CO_2 for the world as a whole by 2050. Malte Meinhausen, professor of climate science at the University of Melbourne and adviser to the IPCC, suggests that we think of a range from 2047 to 2055. Start late or slowly and we have to finish fast and early.

Hold emissions at one-tenth of current levels and we fail to stabilise average global temperatures and end up higher – eventually much higher – than 1.5 degrees. If we continued after 2050 with emissions of 3.7 $GtCO_2$ per annum, equal to one-tenth of the present, temperature after fifty years would exceed 1.5 by 0.3 degrees (Professor Meinhausen suggests a range of 0.19 to 0.43 degrees, with about 0.3 degrees extra for every subsequent half-century).

Of course, it matters what happens to methane and other gases that have a relatively short life in the atmosphere. Alan says that New Zealand has excluded agriculture, with its large methane emissions, from its "net zero" target. Methane has an average life in the atmosphere of about a dozen years, compared with hundreds of years for carbon dioxide. Methane emissions are net zero if we hold them steady at the levels of a dozen or so years ago: as many molecules are being removed from the atmosphere each year as are being added. Reduce absolute methane emissions to zero and atmospheric concentrations will fall gradually to zero during those dozen years. There are relatively straightforward ways to reduce methane emissions. Unlike carbon dioxide, reduction of methane is a source of negative emissions. Far from excluding agriculture from the net-zero objective, New Zealand is seeking to measure its impact scientifically.

Getting to Zero clears up one point of dispute with a number of environmental scientists. In his presentation to the National Press Club on 12 February 2020, Alan argued that gas had a large role to play in balancing intermittent renewable energy – providing power when the sun is not shining and the wind not blowing. Pumped hydro storage and batteries could do the job and eventually would, but gas had a substantial transition role for many decades. Twenty-five people, several of them eminently qualified in atmospheric physics, published a letter in a scholarly journal later in the year, saying that the proposed reliance on gas was inconsistent with holding temperature increases within the 1.5 degree objective. They said that the time had passed for building any new fossil-energy infrastructure, including for power generation from gas.

At the National Press Club, Alan was silent on whether new gas infrastructure should be built. At one point in his address, he said he was aware that building new natural gas generators may be seen as problematic, and that he would come back to that. He didn't come back to it. But he has done so in *Getting to Zero*. Gas has purely a peaking and transitional role. In the quantities implied by that role, there is ample existing gas processing, transportation and power generation infrastructure in place now. Alan has implicitly made the case against investment in new gas infrastructure. The twenty-five scientists should be pleased.

One quibble about language. Alan doesn't like calling carbon dioxide a pollutant, because in moderate concentrations it makes our kind of life possible. Many substances that he would be happy to call pollutants do no harm and some good in suitably low concentrations. I understand that undergraduate engineers are taught that the solution to pollution is dilution. Pollution is the introduction into the environment of a substance which has damaging or unpleasant effects. No doubt about carbon dioxide in concentrations not much higher than they are now! US courts had to adjudicate on the matter about a decade ago, and concluded that carbon dioxide was a pollutant, and therefore subject to regulation by the Environmental Protection Agency.

The economics and policy

Alan's essay is "about the technology, not the policies, which are for our democratically elected political leaders to determine." He notes that governments have "to balance competing priorities across economic growth, scientific advice and community values."

True. But the choice of policy instruments affects how far we can get towards each of several competing objectives. For example, if there were a conflict between economic growth and climate stability, superior policies would give us more of both.

There is no trade-off with scientific and engineering advice; that is what it is, to be understood or not; to be accepted or ignored. Within constraints defined by science and technology, superior policy allows us to eat more cake (economic growth) and to have more left (climate stability).

Laws of economics are as unforgiving as science and technology. Breach them, and the community suffers loss. But much of economics is about optimisation of community value in the light of scientific and technological realities. In the end, some choices among alternative community preferences must be made by political leaders – in our fortunate case, through democratic processes. Australians will do well if we accept the scientific reality as a foundation for choices on climate change mitigation, accept the technological reality to define various paths to emissions reduction, accept the economic realities defining lowest-cost paths to reducing emissions, and in the process clarify any irremovable choices between fundamental objectives. The irreducible choices will mainly involve the distribution of the costs and benefits of change across the community.

There are many advantages in using market exchange to allocate resources across competing uses, wherever conditions exist for effective market competition. That was essential to the victory of Western market over centrally planned economies in the systemic competition through the second half of the twentieth century. But for the optimal supply of public goods – including the electricity transmission networks discussed by Alan – markets don't work and planning is necessary. And they don't work if one firm's activities impose costs or confer benefits on others that are not carried or received by those causing them. This was subject to close analysis in my climate change review, presented to all of Australia's heads of government – federal, state and territory – in 2008.

Networks need to be in public hands, or else their investment and pricing need to be regulated by public authorities. Australia has been slow to learn what is necessary. *Getting to Zero* tells us about the path we have travelled, at least to a position where we can see what needs to be done.

Two kinds of imperfections, in the way costs and benefits of market exchange to society are reflected in private benefits, are important to the transition to zero emissions. Correcting them both with taxes and subsidies or regulation will allow market exchange to drive economic development while achieving required emissions reductions at the lowest possible cost.

One imperfection is that raw market exchange does not value the damage that greenhouse gas emissions from activity impose on others. A tax on emissions, or a subsidy to low-emissions alternatives to established ways of doing things, can reconcile the profit-maximising decisions of businesspeople and the welfare-maximising decisions of citizens with the public interest. In the end, subsidies are paid for by taxes, so the difference is not as great as it may seem at first sight.

After the abolition of the carbon price in 2014, we retained the Renewable Energy Target. Alan notes that it was so successful it led to the costs of solar and wind falling below those of fossil energy, so that it was no longer necessary. Unnecessary in what sense? A new tranche or stronger target would have led to a higher level of output, and lower emissions. Modelling done for the Coalition's own 2014 Warburton review showed that it would have led to lower electricity prices. Unnecessary? Maybe in some sense, but extension of the policy would have led to more cake eaten and more left behind.

The second imperfection is that market exchange does not lead to socially desirable levels of technological and business innovation in the absence of public support. The pioneer produces knowledge that is valuable across the whole of society that she cannot capture for herself. Market exchange without public support does not produce enough innovation. This is especially important when circumstances require rapid technological development – as they do now with climate change.

Correct the market imperfection from greenhouse gas emissions with a carbon price and we can enjoy the magic of markets finding the best trade-offs between cost and emissions reduction. Correct the innovation imperfection with judicious allocation of fiscal subsidies across activities in proportion to the expected value of social benefits and we see an optimal rate of introduction of new ways of doing things.

Our awful history of climate change discussion has ruled out market-based approaches to reducing emissions for the time being. That history carries a high price. There will be a large reward to our standard of living if and when history lifts its veto.

In the meantime, we have to get as far as we can by relying on correcting the imperfections related to innovation. That can be a long way. In some circumstances, the underlying scientific and technological realities mean that deployment of new zero-emissions technology at scale takes costs below those of the old, high-emissions processes. That has happened with solar and wind, and may happen with battery and pumped hydro storage in competition with peaking gas generation. It has happened with supply of electricity for aluminium smelting and may happen for use of zero-emissions hydrogen. But whether or not it happens in any particular case is in the hands of the technological gods.

In some important cases it can never happen. In the words of a song I used to play our grandchildren on a long car journey: "Science is real; you'll never see a unicorn, but you can see a rainbow." No matter what the subsidy for geological capture and storage, it will never be cheaper than releasing carbon dioxide into the atmosphere. Large-scale deployment requires a carbon price or economically equivalent regulation. Public expenditure on technological development is wasted unless it is accompanied or followed by a carbon price or by regulation mandating its use.

In our public discussion at the release in Melbourne of *Getting to Zero*, Alan said that other countries' requirements plus some private companies' preferences for zero-emissions inputs will provide the incentives for deployment of CCS. That requires other governments accepting Australia's free-riding on their carbon price or regulation, or some companies being prepared to accept competitors securing advantage by failing to take similar actions themselves. This is thin ground on which to build a transition strategy.

Larger fiscal subsidies are more likely to push the costs of a new, low-emissions technology below those of the established alternatives. Our subsidies are tiny compared with those of other developed countries. Add up all of the support for low-emissions technologies in the 2021 budget and it may amount to several hundred millions of dollars per year. By contrast, the energy and climate transition subsidies embodied in President Biden's infrastructure package presented to the US Congress in February are proportionally about one hundred times the Australian amount. Other developed countries are closer to the US than the Australian position.

Getting to Zero concludes with an exhortation to "be ambitious, be patient." Be more ambitious and less patient on reducing emissions, and we are more likely to prosper as the energy superpower of the low-carbon world economy.

Ross Garnaut

GETTING TO ZERO

Correspondence

Rebecca Huntley

Alan Finkel has written a comprehensive account of how Australia can transition to renewable energy while still keeping the lights on and standards of living high. His timing is impeccable, as we have seen momentum build for such a vision, despite the pandemic, in all parts of Australian society. Recent research shows 81 per cent of Australians support the Morrison government adopting a net-zero emissions target by 2050, and 87 per cent say they would support accelerating the development of new industries and jobs powered by renewable energy. For anyone, including me, who has learned in piecemeal fashion about the technological and industrial aspects of the shift to renewable technology, this essay provides a must-read, clear and compelling summary of how things work and what's at stake. "The task ahead is, quite simply, immense," Finkel writes. He shows us this mountain to climb and rightly so – I sometimes find it too easy, given my focus on climate change communication and activism, and my sense of the urgency of the task, to forget the scale of the challenge. As my consulting work with people in hard-to-abate industries reminds me, creating a zero-emissions brewery poses different challenges to decarbonising an aluminium smelter.

Finkel also touches on a concern often raised in focus groups I conduct: how can we expand renewables while also protecting our natural environment? "If flooding a valley to build a hydroelectric dam that allows us to close several coal-fired power stations displaces local animals and plants, is that a trade-off that we should favourably consider?" These apparent tensions can be resolved without too much compromise, but the dual challenges of building more renewable infrastructure and preserving our natural environment should always be kept front of mind.

However, as one of the many, many people in what Finkel calls the "fast transition" camp, I am disappointed by the missed opportunity this essay represents. Finkel states that he is an engineer and has written an engineer's essay. But he is being modest. He is far more than that. He has been a senior figure, leader, thinker and public servant in the middle of some of the most important government and policy decisions about energy in Australia over the last decade. He remains a key influencer.

His essay opens with a moving admission that his vision of a net-zero future is inspired by concern for his great-grandchildren, that they might "grow up in a planet just as magnificent as it was when I was young." I empathise. A similar concern led to my current professional and personal commitment to climate change activism. But it's not my great-grandchildren I worry about. It's my children and their peers. Also, to be frank, I worry about myself and my generation. Everyone living in Australia today. The impacts of climate change are being felt now, in extreme weather events, in high temperatures in outer suburbs, in the shrinking islands of the Torres Strait and in the increasingly difficult growing conditions for our farming communities. In recent research into public attitudes, we found that what distinguishes people who are genuinely alarmed and active on the issue of climate change (and Finkel would be among this group) from those who are merely concerned is their response to the question, "How important is climate change to you personally?" Climate change is a real and present danger to people living *today*. Distancing yourself from that allows you to delay action on the issue. And we all know that delay is the new denial. I would add that if we are too timid and drag our feet in this transition, Finkel may not have any great-grandchildren to worry about, given the level of anxiety among younger generations about bringing kids into a world of runaway climate change.

Finkel must know that he will frustrate many by not criticising the lack of consistency and vision shown by politicians and industry leaders on both energy and climate policy. Only Malcolm Roberts gets a serve. Finkel provides a short but swift demolition of the tired but still stubborn arguments of climate change deniers and minimisers. It should be written on cards and handed out on street corners, it's so clear and elegant. And yet he would surely know that these attitudes live on in the conservative parties and even in parts of the ALP. And that such attitudes are why Australia is an international laggard. He wants us to be leading, not "jostling with the hangers-on or mingling with the coalition of the unwilling." But that's exactly where we are – not because of Malcolm Roberts, but because of politicians in mainstream parties. Politicians who continue to be tethered to industries and technologies that no longer serve our national interest. "This essay is about the technology, not the policies, which are for our democratically elected political leaders to determine." Finkel is a leader and a former high-ranking public servant, not a High Court judge. He must have some views on what good policy means for technological advancement and innovation, and how a lack of good policy has frustrated both.

Finkel's essay is full of techno-optimism: "Technology to solve technology's problems." It's certainly the case that participants in my qualitative research get excited when they learn about green steel, battery storage, new developments in solar and, of course, renewable hydrogen – the scale of the decarbonisation project seems less challenging. However, there are limits to technological solutions, which Finkel hints at but doesn't delve into, perhaps because he is not a social scientist. Only policy can drive technological change in the time frame that climate science requires. Furthermore, behavioural change is an important part of the zero-emission goal. We can pursue the dual goals of decarbonisation and prosperity, but a different version of prosperity might be forced upon us, given the level of warming we've already reached and the trajectory we are on. Things have been lost and will continue to be lost. I would have loved some reflection by Finkel on how we might learn to live in a world that's been damaged by climate change and will continue to be.

Given my research has recently focused on public attitudes to gas, I was particularly interested in Finkel's commentary on this area. The concern I have is that his position could be framed as an argument that we need a greater supply of gas, which would involve more expensive infrastructure and opening up new gas basins – even to continue the damaging practice of fracking, which has been opposed by environmentalists and farmers in coalition. Of course, this framing is not entirely under Finkel's control. Those who are determined to keep the fossil-fuel industries alive at any cost will misrepresent any commentary from such an esteemed expert to argue for gas's ongoing role. Finkel has, in his essay and in his commentary generally, focused on gas for peaking. But this is strategically ignored by those arguing for "a gas-led transition" or that new gas is essential to the expansion of renewables. There are more than a few sober commentators on energy transition in this country who are prepared to argue that Australia doesn't need new gas. Finkel's position risks capture and manipulation by those who seek to prolong our dependence on a polluting energy source that we cannot rely on to secure our nation's economic future.

Despite my criticisms, there is no doubt Finkel's personal vision for a future net-zero-emissions society is one that many can share. He asks us to be ambitious and patient. Seventy-two per cent of Australians agree with the statement "Climate change is something we need to act on now." In the focus groups I conduct there is a sense of impatience and frustration across the board that the world seems to be moving and we are being left behind. It is a time for ambition. The time for patience has passed.

Rebecca Huntley

GETTING
TO ZERO

Correspondence

Nick Rowley

For anyone who has endured what passes for debate on climate change and emissions reduction in Australia, Alan Finkel's forward-looking, largely optimistic and rigorous presentation of the elements of Australia's required transition to a net-zero energy economy is a refreshing and at times exciting read.

How nice to now understand how and why wind turbines require three blades, and the various methods whereby electric vehicles can be charged slowly, quickly or – if you are lucky – very quickly. And who could fail to be thrilled at the prospects for a country not only so richly endowed with wind and solar resources crying out to be harnessed, but also now potentially on the cusp of developing a whole new zero- or low-emissions industry based on hydrogen?

Alan is more than across the technical detail. He is genuinely enthused by the challenges of climate change and marshalling the forces required to address them. The task of achieving net zero is indeed immense. It is something no economy has ever achieved or tried to achieve. It means overhauling existing energy, industry, agriculture and transport systems, which are established, employ people and largely add to emissions. But Finkel does not let the magnitude of the task dissuade him from understanding the technologies required to achieve it.

Yet it will take more than "technology to solve technology's problems." Finkel's hero, Buckminster Fuller, can no doubt teach us much, but we must beware magic-pudding thinking. No technology emerges in a vacuum. Much of it relies on public policy, public funding and a suite of additional incentives. Achieving net zero within the required time frame must involve policies that deliver a "just measure of pain" to the existing fossil-fuel infrastructure that is intensifying the climate problem. To ignore this, as Finkel does, is to neglect much of the challenge we face.

And yet I am with Alan in his frustration with those who wish achieving net-zero emissions were somehow straightforward. Climate advocates who argue that

Australia must reach this target by 2035 are, sadly, whistling in the wind – or "dreamin'," as the Michael Caton character said in the classic Australian film *The Castle*. If you are serious about achieving a net-zero economy, you must be at ease with the complexity of achieving change that goes to the heart of our political economy and replacing the high-carbon infrastructure on which we all rely.

The job of chief scientist, which Finkel occupied for five years until last November, is hard at the best of times. Where science meets policy will always be a place of tension. Politics is concerned not with positive questions, but with collective decisions and action: not "What is true?" but "What shall we do?" Because many of the questions most relevant to policy decisions may not or cannot have scientifically informed answers, politics challenges science. During the COVID-19 pandemic, we saw chief medical officers Brendan Murphy and Paul Kelly standing side by side with Scott Morrison, but even in response to the pandemic, Murphy and Kelly could only inform, not make, what are rightly political decisions.

An effective chief scientist can be a powerful scientific voice in policy debates. But they must walk a fine line, disentangling policy debate into clear questions and establishing which of these relate to scientific knowledge and which to our values, hopes and political principles. This is particularly hard when it comes to climate change. The link between carbon emissions, our existing means of generating energy and Australia's clear vulnerability to the smorgasbord of climate risks – physical, environmental, economic and social – makes it particularly hard for even the most disciplined scientist not to spell out the all too human (and political) implications of failing to develop and implement effective climate policy.

During my time at the Downing Street Policy Directorate between 2004 and 2006, I worked closely with Sir David King, then the United Kingdom's chief scientist. I was charged with advising Prime Minister Tony Blair and guiding UK efforts on climate change in the lead-up to the 2005 G8 summit: the first time a leader had made climate change a key priority for heads of state. In my policy work, I could get ambition, adjectives and rhetoric from any climate advocate on any day of the week. What King and scientists such as Sir John Houghton (who advised Margaret Thatcher, established the Hadley Centre for Climate Science and Services, and led efforts to establish the Intergovernmental Panel on Climate Change) could deliver were numbers – the specific emissions reductions required to reduce climate risk, domestically and globally – which allowed the government to develop and argue for more ambitious policies and legislation.

King was respected. He had been integral to the government response to the vicious outbreak of mad cow disease three years earlier. But just two months before I started work in the office above Number 10's black door, he damagingly overstepped the mark on climate change, commenting that it was "a more serious threat to the world than terrorism." Climate advocates might have been pleased by the chief scientist's bravura, but so soon after the 9/11 attacks, Washington was deeply offended. King was persona non grata in the US capital, and his insensitivity stunted Blair's efforts to argue for progressive climate policy with President George W. Bush. It took months of diplomatic effort with Bush and those around him for the White House even to countenance serious discussion of how to strengthen the international climate response.

In contrast, King's immediate predecessor in the role, the Australian scientist (and champion of the now famous "R number" so useful in understanding the spread of infectious disease) Lord Robert May, played a powerfully supportive role: using science to strengthen diplomatic effort. As president of the Royal Society, May led and orchestrated the first joint statement from the G8 science academies on the need for a more effective response to the climate problem. Their concise statement cut through: diplomats seeking to play down climate risk could be reminded, publicly or behind closed doors, of the statement signed by the president of their own leading science academy. This was science powerfully helping to build political and policy ambition.

For Finkel, there is only distraction to be had in looking backwards, but plenty to inspire us looking forwards. His concern is the future. Each page of his essay brings reasoned hope that achieving net-zero emissions is both possible and highly desirable. Surely our path needs more go signs and fewer stop signs. But, sadly, if we – as Finkel does – see climate response in the coming decade as having the potential to be every bit as exciting as space exploration in the 1960s, we ignore the key missing ingredient: political will.

Much as I would like to believe that Finkel is right, his optimism is naively blind to Australia's current domestic politics. Our future is affected by our past. Look back and we can see the political and policy mess of the past fifteen years. Depressingly, Australia's current climate-policy confusion goes beyond the position of the Morrison government. We are now at a point where both major parties favour a so-called "gas-led recovery" and will not rule out new coal-fired power stations. Any statements from our political leaders on the need to achieve a net-zero economy are meaningless if they continue to support new fossil-fuel infrastructure. They might as well tout the benefits of a healthy diet and exercise while ordering the double burger, large chips and a super-sized sugary drink.

The excitement of space exploration in the 1960s was founded on political leadership driving national purpose. Although NASA was created in 1958, it was

President John F. Kennedy's "We choose to go the moon" speech in September 1962 that led to the Mercury, Gemini and Apollo programs. This was no "sentence or two" in a speech as a means to avoid international criticism, it was an unequivocal national priority backed by institutions, policy and money. With the average age of those employed on Apollo being just twenty-six, a whole generation was enthused. Between 1964 and 1966, public investment in NASA's work amounted to around 4 per cent of the federal budget. When Neil Armstrong first set foot on the moon, the moment was televised live, alongside that key quote from Kennedy's speech.

John Fitzgerald Kennedy and Alexander Boris de Pfeffel Johnson may have little in common, but Johnson has made achieving net zero a core priority for the United Kingdom, influencing economic decisions and the diplomatic positioning of "global Britain" after Brexit. Contrast Scott Morrison's tokenistic words with the serious political and policy commitment of his UK counterpart. The Johnson government has just laid an order before parliament to enshrine a new carbon target in law by the end of June 2021. The United Kingdom's existing target of a 68 per cent reduction of 1990 emissions levels by 2030 is the highest set by any country under the Paris Agreement. Now under the new laws it will aim to achieve a 78 per cent reduction by 2035, while also incorporating the carbon emissions contributed by the United Kingdom's international aviation and shipping. Our prime minister might not believe in targets, but Johnson clearly does. The British prime minister is also willing to be legally bound by them, and supports them with policy informed by the independent Climate Change Committee, together with an ambitious ten-point plan to achieve net zero.

The development of technology does not and can never occur in a policy vacuum. As the economist Mariana Mazzucato shows so brilliantly, smartphones were not solely dreamed up by entrepreneurial tech wizards in garages. They were the result of government decisions in the form of focused public investment and subsidy. And we can thank the CSIRO – Australia's own publicly funded scientific research institution – for the development of the wi-fi that the world has relied on to stay connected through the COVID-19 pandemic. As much as I would like to purchase an electric vehicle – as I am sure many other Australians would – I cannot afford any of the comparatively few cars available here. The paucity of options has everything to do with politics and the resulting lack of policy. It has nothing to do with technology. UK consumers receive a generous grant of £2500 ($4500) towards the price of a new electric car. This year, Volkswagen plans to sell around 450,000 electric vehicles globally, not one of which will be in Australia.

In his current role as adviser to the government on low emissions, Finkel cannot absent himself from the politics of climate change, even though he might like to. Rather than using his rigorous scientific, engineering and technological know-how to help build a more effective political and policy response, Finkel's wide-eyed enthusiasm for technological solutions to the climate crisis runs the risk of supporting and legitimising the very rhetoric and politics that got Australia into its current woeful climate position.

Being deaf to the politics of climate change does not mean you can remove yourself from it. Bolstering the likes of Senator Matt Canavan and energy minister Angus Taylor sadly serves to legitimise their – weak at best, hostile at worst – stance on the net-zero outcome Finkel is so enthusiastic about delivering. That Finkel quotes the prime minister's recent half-hearted rhetoric on reaching "net-zero emissions as soon as possible, and preferably by 2050" leaves the reader confused. The 2019 National Hydrogen Strategy and the 2020 Low Emissions Technology Statement might serve to give the current "emperor" some policy "clothes," but Finkel must realise that the economic transition required to achieve a national energy switch of this scale demands far more than funding for research into new technologies (vital though that is). Context is everything, and as uplifting as technology optimism can be, it must not be blind to it.

Finkel is, perhaps, the Anthony Fauci of Australian domestic energy and climate policy. Amid the noise – lumps of coal being brandished in parliament, prime ministers being "rolled," and statements likening the promotion of electric vehicles to a "war on the weekend" – he has remained calm, considered and committed to the job at hand.

Part of what stultifies our climate politics is a lack of optimism and imagination. Some of that Finkel brings in spades. No one person can be everything: negotiating internal and external politics, contributing to policy, and appreciating and promoting the technologies that must be brought to bear at scale. I recall Robert May once sharing with me that almost everything he knew about being chief scientist and advising the government on scientific matters he learned from playing chess. I don't know if Alan Finkel plays the game. But if he does, my sense is he plays it well.

Nick Rowley

Correspondence

Richie Merzian

In responding to this essay, I feel the best place to start is where Professor Finkel ended: "be ambitious; be patient." After accompanying Professor Finkel on a long and well-structured journey through the complexities, pitfalls and opportunities of climate change, we are told to cool our jets. Or, in the Australian vernacular, that she'll be right.

It left me conflicted. This year, global energy-related carbon dioxide emissions are predicted to rise by 1.5 billion tonnes – the second-largest increase in history. We do not have the luxury of time, or, as the United States' Special Envoy for Climate Change, John Kerry, put it recently, to be "willy-nilly" with the next ten years of the "gargantuan" climate fight. Not long after this essay was published, the United States and China, the world's two largest polluters, committed to tackling the climate crisis "with the seriousness and urgency that it demands." The overwhelming global narrative is "urgency." With our oversized carbon footprint, we are in the top 10 per cent of countries for high emissions and the third-largest exporter of fossil fuels in the world. The question has to be asked: where the bloody hell is Australia? Right now, the Australian government does not treat climate change urgently – or seriously. While other countries are sprinting, Prime Minister Morrison is being dragged towards committing to a net-zero time frame. Australia's "long-term emissions reduction strategy" remains wholly elusive. All we know from the prime minister is that the path won't be linear, meaning the majority of climate action will be pushed to the 2040s. And so it is worrying that in this essay we have an "energy transition" without a time frame or trajectory.

Professor Finkel goes to great lengths to frame himself as both technologically and politically agnostic. Setting the scene early, he defines himself in quick succession as "technology-neutral," as centrist in the "fast" and "slow" transition debate, and then for good measure he scatters a handful of "green" credentials into the mix: co-founder of a green lifestyle magazine, investor in low-emissions technology stocks and electric vehicle owner (he owns two, actually). But let's be clear: Professor Finkel works for the federal government. His new position as a "special adviser" on low-emissions (not zero-emissions) technologies continues much of the advocacy of his last public-sector job, as chief scientist.

That role elevated Professor Finkel to the national stage. In fact Morrison went a step further and elevated him to the international stage, mentioning Professor Finkel by name at President Joe Biden's climate summit on 22 April 2021. His credibility comes with the lab coat: "chief scientist" suggests he is independent and will fearlessly deliver robust, peer-reviewed advice. The same people sceptical of Scott Morrison's strident fossil-fuel evangelism could be forgiven for picking up Finkel's essay and interpreting it as a rational, independent argument for a gas-led recovery.

The problem is that the role of chief scientist has never been independent. It is a contract position with no statutory underpinnings and a history of controversy related to conflicts of interest and impartiality. Various calls to make it a statutory position have failed (including a 2004 Senate inquiry into the management of conflicts of interest, which was pretty much ignored).

In 2004, Professor Robin Batterham, then Australia's chief scientist, came under scrutiny for concurrently occupying the role of chief technologist for Rio Tinto. Professor Batterham's publicly funded office was administered out of his Rio Tinto office, with exactly the same staff (Rio Tinto was reimbursed for the costs of providing staff for that support). I doubt this is news to Professor Finkel, given it appears from the acknowledgments that Professor Batterham reviewed and commented on his essay.

In 2011, just halfway through a five-year appointment as chief scientist, Professor Penny Sackett resigned from the post amid reports that innovation minister Kim Carr found her "too outspoken and opinionated, and felt she did not give sufficient regard to Labor's agenda and the processes of government." These reports were denied by Carr.

Since he was appointed chief scientist, Finkel has been widely criticised for his support of gas, and in this essay he responds to a public rebuke on this issue by twenty-five leading scientists. If Finkel were still chief scientist, the essay – an endorsement of the government's technology roadmap, hydrogen plan and gas-led recovery – would make a lot more sense. Instead, we have a clever and subtle piece of political writing about the positive role of fossil fuels in solving Australia's energy and emissions problems – overtly, with references to gas, and covertly, with arguments for "blue" hydrogen, a Trojan horse for gas and coal, premised on the magic of carbon capture and storage (CCS).

The arguments against gas have been well ventilated by the Australia Institute in other forums, and so I will focus here on hydrogen and CCS. Professor Finkel has been called an "evangelist" for hydrogen since 2018, when he led the development of an enthusiastic sixty-page briefing called *Hydrogen for Australia's Future*, which promoted hydrogen as Australia's "next big export." This led to an official National Hydrogen Strategy and a rush to develop Australia's hydrogen industry with a $300 million fund.

The Australia Institute found that the National Hydrogen Strategy dramatically overestimated the global demand for hydrogen by implying that demand from the two largest markets, Japan and South Korea, was significantly higher (in one case by a factor of eleven) than their official targets. Professor Finkel admits in the essay that Japanese demand for imported hydrogen was quite modest when the strategy was agreed upon. But with these inflated numbers in view, the rush was on to service the prospective markets. And the cheapest and most widely available way to do so was with hydrogen made from fossil fuels. Currently, most hydrogen produced globally is generated with fossil fuels, producing around 830 million tonnes of emissions per year (the equivalent of the combined emissions of the United Kingdom and Indonesia), and there is nothing clean about it.

While hydrogen *does* have potential as a zero-emissions fuel, this is the case only when it is produced from water using electrolysis. What is problematic – and highly misleading – is using the term "clean hydrogen," as Professor Finkel does, to collectively describe hydrogen produced from water (green hydrogen) and hydrogen produced from fossil fuels (blue hydrogen).

Professor Finkel should have recognised Senator Matt Canavan's strong support for his National Hydrogen Strategy as a red flag, not a glowing endorsement. Canavan is an enthusiastic proponent of fossil fuels in any form. If a politician who calls himself "Mr Coal" and happily co-opts the Black Lives Matter movement with a "Black Coal Matters" bumper sticker shows affection for your "low-emissions" technology, be wary.

Professor Finkel claims emissions generated from the production of hydrogen using fossil fuels can be captured and buried underground by CCS. While CCS is mentioned several times in the essay, the actual process and history of CCS is glossed over. The technology was originally pioneered by (you guessed it) the fossil fuel industry as a way of enhancing oil extraction by pumping carbon dioxide into depleted wells to recover more oil. Another component was added to the process to help address climate change: the wells or any other geological storage are plugged so as to keep the carbon dioxide underground and out of the atmosphere.

If this sounds familiar, it should. The proponents of "clean hydrogen" world-wide are trying to resurrect the corpse of the long-dead and long-ago debunked idea of "clean coal." Clean coal is a myth that has been propagated by (yep, you guessed it again) the fossil-fuel industry for decades, whereby the carbon emissions from burning coal are captured before they are released into the atmosphere and buried underground. Despite decades of support, including more than $1.3 billion from Australian governments since 2003, there isn't a single commercial CCS facility for coal. Even the coal companies themselves have moved on. In 2017, the then CEO of US-based coalmining company American Consolidated Natural Resources admitted that the whole idea of "clean coal" was a fallacy, and the CCS industry fund, COAL21, has in recent years shifted spending from research and development into advertising, including the infamous "little black rock" campaign.

Professor Finkel's faith in CCS to clean hydrogen is idealistic, given it has failed to clean coal. As he explains, there are only nineteen large-scale operational CCS facilities worldwide. The only local example is Chevron's Gorgon gas project in Western Australia, which is still not fully operational. The project was only approved on the condition that CCS would be used to bury 40 per cent of the project's carbon emissions over a five-year period, but storage did not start until 2019 – three years after production began. Even now, the $3.1 billion system is not working properly, and it has resulted in millions of tonnes of emissions being released – roughly equivalent to the emissions from a year's worth of domestic flights in Australia. While the project received more than $60 million in government funding, Chevron has not faced any penalty for breaching the terms of its approval. Despite the collective failure of all CCS projects in Australia, in April 2021 the federal government announced $539.2 million of further investment in clean hydrogen and CCS.

It seems that CCS does not have to prove itself to benefit from unwavering government support. Of all possible technologies available and forthcoming to address climate change, CCS was elevated to the top five in the federal government's Low Emissions Technology Investment Roadmap, which Professor Finkel led. Was it elevated because of the potential emission reductions from CCS over the next twenty years? Not according to the Department of Energy. It admitted during Senate Estimates that it does not expect any emissions reductions from CCS between now and 2040. And yet this is the technology Professor Finkel deems necessary for our hydrogen future.

On closer inspection, Professor Finkel doesn't really have any good reason to push fossil-fuel hydrogen. He claims an "in-principle" concern for fuel diversity (which sounds eerily like energy minister Angus Taylor's claim that "we need more horses in the race", as long as those horses are fossil fuels). He claims producing renewable hydrogen is "inherently inefficient" compared to using fossil fuels. This seems ridiculous, given that fossil-fuel hydrogen with CCS requires burying commercial levels of carbon dioxide underground forever, an impossible task in Australia to date.

He claims the "cost of capturing the carbon dioxide is essentially free, such as hydrogen production from fossil fuels." Nowhere does he explain how it is "essentially free," and all experience to date tells us that it is prohibitively expensive to permanently store high levels of captured carbon. And who is obligated to ensure the gas is stored permanently and safely, given the federal and state governments have agreed to take on liability for the Gorgon CCS project after fifteen years?

In the end, Professor Finkel admits that CCS has not been proven to be commercially viable. Investing in unproven technology is a luxury you can afford only when time is of no concern. Without a clear deadline for Australia's transition to net-zero emissions, we continue to fund failed technologies repeatedly.

Professor Finkel calls on all to "be ambitious, be patient." But his essay is not ambitious, and science shows we cannot afford to be patient. Professor Finkel has provided an eloquent and engaging sales pitch. But he is selling a failed product: the technologies deemed acceptable by a government that lacks credibility on climate action. And in this decisive decade, we can't afford to back the wrong horse.

Richie Merzian

GETTING TO ZERO

Correspondence

Ben Wilson

I have had the privilege to work with Alan Finkel as part of the advisory panel for the National Hydrogen Strategy and, more recently, as a member of the ministerial council for the Technology Investment Roadmap, which Alan chairs.

Dr Finkel's article is a first-class discussion of the challenges and opportunities presented by Australia's energy transition. I recommend it to anyone looking to cut through the mixed-quality debate on this topic.

We all bring a personal perspective to the challenges of climate change and humankind's response to it. I grew up as a voracious reader of science fiction – "hard SF," the kind where the laws of physics are obeyed – and in particular the works of the great twentieth-century sci-fi authors Isaac Asimov and Arthur C. Clarke. In their books, humankind has often migrated throughout the solar system or across the galaxy. The future is mostly utopian: many of the social problems of contemporary society seem no longer to exist. The advance of technology has continued to transform lives, almost always for the better. Sometimes the future Earth is portrayed as a kind of nature reserve: with a small human population and returned to its former natural glory. Climate change, of course, is almost never mentioned; it was not a focus before the late twentieth century. My childhood reading and scientific education left me with a core belief that technology, innovation and the application of human endeavour and ingenuity is the best way to solve our problems, including the pressing need to decarbonise our energy system and achieve net zero.

In 2015, I moved to Australia from the United Kingdom, where I was a senior executive at UK Power Networks, the country's largest electricity distributor. I came to run Australian Gas Networks, now known as the Australian Gas Infrastructure Group, which is Australia's largest owner of natural gas distribution networks. There are many similarities between running an electricity grid in the United Kingdom and a gas grid in Australia, so it was the differences that struck me most. Most importantly: what was the plan to stay in business? We distribute fossil fuel in a world that is moving towards net zero. For electricity distribution, the energy transition comes under the category of an interesting challenge: renewables penetration is disrupting the operation of the electricity system, but no one really thinks we will do without electricity networks in the future. For a natural gas network, however, the threat is existential: to use the metaphor of former Nokia CEO Stephen Elop, we sit on a "burning platform." If we don't find a way to decarbonise, then customers will find alternative solutions, potentially well before 2050.

In 2015, the threat didn't seem quite so urgent, but I could see that it would come soon enough, and so I looked around for a solution. At that time, our UK sister company, Northern Gas Networks, was working on a project called H21 Leeds. The study looked at the feasibility of converting the natural gas network of the city of Leeds, in northern England, to run entirely on zero-carbon hydrogen. Almost immediately, I could see that this provided the answer we were looking for. In principle, there is no reason why we cannot deliver hydrogen through gas networks for customers to use as they use natural gas today. Burning hydrogen produces only water vapour, and if it is produced from electrolysis of water, using renewable electricity (green hydrogen), or from methane, with carbon capture and storage (blue hydrogen), then there are no carbon dioxide emissions from production.

We moved quickly to turn this idea into reality. This started with "Gas Vision 2050," a report published in 2017. It laid out an ambitious plan for the gas sector with three stages: first, studies and pilot projects ("make hydrogen a thing"); second, large-scale blending of green hydrogen into existing natural gas networks ("make hydrogen plan A"); and, third, full-scale conversion of the gas networks to green and blue hydrogen ("make hydrogen business-as-usual"). Stage one is complete, and stage two is now the focus, to be completed this decade. We aim to achieve stage three, full system conversion, by 2040.

When you have a burning platform, you need to work fast, and we certainly have. Pilot projects are now in operation across Australia, including our own hydrogen park, a 1.25 megawatt electrolyser (Australia's largest), which is blending green hydrogen into the local gas network and supplying pure green hydrogen to industrial customers. It seems as if a new hydrogen project is announced every week, and some of our largest industrial companies are mobilising behind this emerging economic sector. Dr Finkel's work and communication skills have been absolutely key in building the momentum we now see for hydrogen.

The rapid growth of interest in hydrogen in Australia, from almost nothing five years ago, is just one example of the fundamental force I referred to earlier: human ingenuity, which will drive the technological change that can solve our problems. Technological advances, combined with our natural competitive advantages in Australia, including abundant solar and wind resources, allow us to meet the challenges of climate change and create new national opportunities. One example is green hydrogen, which offers us a way to store and transport our renewable power, and could make us an exporting superpower of renewable energy in a decade or two, in the way we are today with natural gas, coking coal and iron ore.

More than two centuries ago, Thomas Malthus forecast that the clash between constant population growth and limited food production would lead to disaster. Technological advances have deferred this scenario, but our ever-growing energy consumption and the earth's finite ability to cope with atmospheric carbon dioxide is another Malthusian trap. But as with food production, human ingenuity can harness technological change to avoid catastrophe.

Unlike the authors I read growing up, twenty-first-century science fiction writers do address climate change. In Kim Stanley Robinson's novel 2312, humans have spread throughout the solar system and are pushing on to the stars. Earth is at least two degrees hotter, but the damage stopped years ago, and attempts at repair are underway. In Robinson's book, the first half of our century is referred to as "the Dithering," and future generations wonder what took us so long to fix the problem!

Until Elon Musk and others like him can transport us through the solar system, this planet is all we have. We need to take care of it. I am convinced that technology, human ingenuity in action, will enable us to make the energy transition to net zero – by 2050 or before. This will create new and exciting opportunities for Australia.

Ben Wilson

Correspondence

Ian McAuley

"My approach stems partly from my background as an engineer," Alan Finkel writes. While his last official position was chief scientist, his first degree and his PhD were in electrical engineering. Wherever our subsequent work and study may take us, our education in our formative years tends to shape our way of thinking. His approach to the issue – how to reduce our energy sector's contribution to greenhouse gas emissions – is that of an engineer.

Once the problem or opportunity is defined, the engineer has two tasks. One is to apply science to achieve practical outcomes; the other is to communicate with those who have the authority to implement his or her ideas. In a democracy, that means reaching out not only to the lawmakers and budget-holders in executive government, but also to the public that votes them into office. That is difficult in any area involving disruptive change, and it is particularly difficult in dealing with climate change, because to most people the threat does not appear to be imminent, and because much of our material prosperity has been based on a carbon-intensive economy. It is too easy for the issue to be framed as the false dichotomy of "economy" versus "environment."

Although he starts with some facts about global warming – a short and clear summary of the science of climate change, just in case anyone needs convincing – he soon moves on to describe how Australia's energy sector can be transformed to contribute to a clean-energy future. This is Finkel the engineer writing, explaining in clear terms the technologies that can decarbonise the sector, from the basics of how electrons carry energy, to the reasons wind turbines always have three blades.

While many analysts take a sector-by-sector approach to emissions reduction, Finkel centres his case on electricity. He says, don't stop at decarbonising electricity: expand low-cost electricity generated from sunlight and wind to electrify transport and to develop a hydrogen economy, reaching into other sectors such as steel.

With a little editing – if he replaced his personal anecdotes with the language of bureaucracy, for instance – this essay could serve as the government's green paper on "Australia's Energy Transition" – that is, if our government were willing to engage with the public on difficult public policy problems through the traditional green paper/white paper process.

Of course public servants preparing a green paper would always be aware of the demands of their masters and guided by political sensitivities: we see this in Defence, where "climate change" is on a list of forbidden terms. Although Finkel is no longer chief scientist, he has been appointed a special adviser to the government on low-emissions technology, and his essay displays the caution of a public servant. He does have a couple of digs at politicians – at Senator Malcolm Roberts, for misunderstanding trend data, and at Scott Morrison, indirectly, for his silly comments on electric vehicles in the 2019 election campaign. But these are minor criticisms, and for the most part he goes along with the Commonwealth's agenda on energy and climate – to the extent that a set of talking points lacking any coherent principles could be described as an "agenda."

Finkel's political sensitivity shows in two areas of his essay: one is the omission of discussion about the energy sector's contribution to greenhouse gases. The essay includes time-series data on temperature trends, electricity production and energy consumption, presented in clear graphic form. As one turns the pages, it would be reasonable to expect a similar graph showing the energy sector's contribution to greenhouse gases – the essential theme of his essay – but the graph isn't there. So, drawing on Australian government data, I include my own graph opposite.

Had Finkel included such a graph, he could hardly have avoided explaining why emissions declined from 2012 to 2014 – the period when there was a price on carbon – and subsequently resumed their growth. He only mentions carbon pricing once, and that is in the specific context of generating electricity from biomass (it's too expensive). In a document of this nature, it is reasonable to concentrate on technologies and costs – without considering funding. But Finkel makes clear his support for market forces, and what could be a clearer use of market forces than placing a price on carbon? Carbon pricing goes some way towards accounting for the externalities in burning fossil fuels: it is essentially a cost of production. (The government's mantra is about "technology, not taxes," but even if carbon pricing were collected by the ATO as a payment for resource use, it would no more be a "tax" than a road toll is a "tax.")

The other way Finkel shows deference to the government's agenda is by retreating into bureaucratic vagueness about the role of natural gas, which he sees as playing a "firming" role in electricity supply – that is, it could supply electricity when there is a shortfall in wind and solar electricity.

No one denies the need for firming. In any electricity system, when there is a sudden change in supply or demand, there has to be a mechanism to stop the voltage and frequency from running out of control. Power-system managers have always had to be nimble enough to cope with unexpected outages of power lines or sudden demands by big users. But why does Finkel seem to assume gas has to play that role? The need for firming can be reduced somewhat if we invest in high-voltage transmission lines to connect the widely dispersed renewable energy zones identified in the Integrated System Plan prepared by the Australian Energy Market Operator (AEMO). The wind can be blowing in North Queensland when a high-pressure system becalms Victoria under a heavy fog; the sun can still be shining on the west coast of South Australia while it is setting in Sydney, and peak demand for electricity is building up on the east coast. Transmission lines are expensive, but they will still be operating when gas pipelines have become stranded assets.

Also, Finkel tends to focus on the supply side of firming, making only passing reference to demand-side firming, which involves temporarily reducing the load

Figure 1: Emissions from energy sector, Australia, September 2001 to September 2020

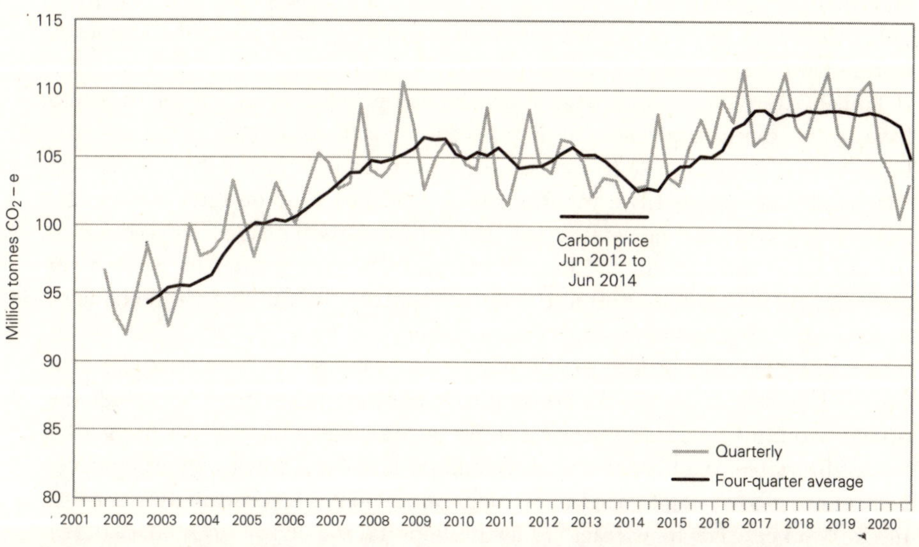

Source: Data source: Australian Government, Quarterly Update of Australia's National Greenhouse Gas Inventory, September 2020

on the grid when its supply side is stressed. Internet-based technologies, combined with wise market design, can do a great deal of demand-side firming – for example, by turning on people's water heaters during periods when there is a temporary surge in rooftop-generated solar electricity.

While a diversified spread of renewable resources can ease the need for firming, there are means of effectively storing electricity to cope with sudden changes in demand or supply. Pumped hydro systems have been with us ever since the Tumut power stations in the Snowy Mountains Scheme were completed in 1973, and there are old open-pit mine sites and other places that are suitable to be developed for pumped hydro, albeit with major investments in earthworks, generators and transmission lines. Batteries, however, are changing the way we go about firming. There is nothing new about using batteries to store electricity – remote farms and other settlements were using 32-volt battery systems seventy years ago. But over the past few years, they have become bigger and more affordable. Most importantly, unlike pumped hydro systems, which take years to develop and have their own environmental costs, batteries can be installed with short lead times.

Initially the role of big batteries, such as the Hornsdale battery in South Australia, was to provide very short-term stabilisation of the electricity grid, but increasingly they are being used for longer-term storage. The other developments emerging are electric cars ("batteries on wheels") – which are stationary most of the time and can help balance supply and demand – and affordable domestic storage batteries, "behind the meter."

Finkel covers these technological developments in his essay, but he seems to have a very conservative view on their potential for firming; instead, he sees natural gas as filling this role for some time to come. He suggests there would be "negligible" emissions from gas, because it would be used on only a few occasions over a year, and he asserts that "market forces will ensure that the use of natural gas is minimised." That's not unreasonable: it's similar to the way an environmentally conscious remote community that is off the grid would be wise to have a diesel generator as an insurance policy.

But if we need so little capacity, why does Finkel not rule out the idea that gas-fired power plants should be built to serve this purpose, even though the AEMO, working on conservative assumptions, calculates that for gas to be economically viable, the long-run price would need to be as low as $4 a gigajoule, and charging costs would need to be high. Although gas is plentiful, it is becoming very expensive to extract. Is he perhaps taking it for granted that the government will go ahead with a highly subsidised gas-fired power station, regardless of the cost–benefit economics?

In this part of the essay, Finkel departs from his otherwise clear style: it appears he has slipped into the role of the public servant who avoids going against expert advice but still gives his or her political master enough wriggle room to implement their preferred policies. This is more than a matter of semantics, because a great deal is at stake – a vast amount of public money, a large and expensive stranded asset and possible retaliatory trade measures against Australia if we continue to lag on decarbonising our economy. If there is excess capacity in a gas-fired power station, that capacity will be used: even if its owners cannot cover full costs, they will dump electricity at marginal cost, worsening emissions.

Finkel could have rewritten the section on firming to suggest a way for the government to save face while backing down from its proposals to build a 1000-megawatt gas-fired power station to replace Liddell, and to develop new coal-seam gas fields in Narrabri and the Beetaloo Basin. There is already plenty of gas available to run peaking gas generators: as he says, these generators would operate only for a "small number of hours." But he bypasses this opportunity to rescue the government from its economic folly.

Nevertheless, Finkel's essay is a valuable contribution to our understanding of the industrial transformation involved in moving to a decarbonised energy sector. To his credit, Finkel dismisses the idea that dealing effectively with climate change will be accompanied by a hit to our economy: this is "flawed thinking," he writes. Finkel trusts the Australian people to understand the science and engineering of that transformation. Our politicians, particularly those in executive government, seem to think the public do not need to know about the technicalities of energy. Finkel's essay is the green paper the government should have produced before jumping into its "gas-fired recovery."

Ian McAuley

Hugh Saddler

Alan Finkel's essay opens with an excellent, brief account of how atmospheric carbon dioxide affects climate and how the facts show precisely why those who reject this science are wrong. The remainder of the essay sets out his assessment of which technologies will most effectively enable Australia to transition to net-zero greenhouse gas emissions. Finkel is a very good technology writer. The text is consistently readable, while almost always achieving the difficult feat of being simultaneously precise, accurate and concise. To summarise it, the pathway to the zero-emissions energy supply system that Finkel advocates consists of three major components. The first is 100 per cent renewable electricity generation (he correctly considers nuclear generation to be a "non-starter" for Australia), supported by a combination of battery, pumped hydro and hydrogen-based storage. The second is a combination of electrical technologies and hydrogen for all thermal energy requirements. The third is a combination of battery electric and hydrogen fuel cell power for transport and other mobile equipment. Most well-informed commentators would broadly agree with this pathway.

Finkel's account, of course, goes into far more detail about energy supply technologies than my summary suggests. One way he achieves readability is to present a single narrative, seldom acknowledging the existence of differing views and current debates about some of the particular technology choices he advocates. As well as achieving readability, the single narrative is probably a necessary consequence of his overall approach of focusing on "the technology, not the policies, which are for our democratically elected political leaders to determine." Unfortunately, the separation between technology choices and policy choices is not as distinct as his words imply, which creates problems for the essay.

The essay is certainly political, in the broadest sense, because of the way Finkel goes about the entirely appropriate task of persuading his readers. Unfortunately, at several points, it degenerates into what is best described as heavy-handed debating tactics. For example, early in the essay Finkel states, in an apparent attempt to be positive and encouraging about the coming energy system transition, that "the good news is that there is momentum. From 2005 to 2018, the OECD countries cut emissions by an average of 9 per cent, Australia by 13 per cent." Australian emissions did indeed fall, but entirely because of dramatic reductions from the land sector. Energy combustion emissions increased by 6 per cent from 2005 to 2016, before levelling off in 2017 and 2018. As a share of Australia's total emissions, they increased from 58 per cent in 2005 to 71 per cent in 2018. If, as Finkel states, emissions are the only really important performance indicator for the energy transition (an absolutely correct assessment), Australia has, as yet, no momentum at all. (Energy emissions fell in 2019–20, but almost entirely because of the dramatic negative impact of the pandemic lockdowns on consumption of petroleum fuels for road transport and aviation.)

A little further on, Finkel seeks to present himself as holding the reasonable middle ground between "some at one end of the debate who want no change at all, and others at the other end who want to move faster than is feasible." This grossly oversimplifies the diverse array of positions advanced by participants in Australia's energy emissions policy debate.

Finkel later singles out for explicit criticism one group of debate participants as being, by implication, part of the faster-than-feasible cohort. The group in question comprised twenty-five scientists who wrote him an open letter taking issue with his public support for gas generation. (I was one of the twenty-five.) However, what they objected to was not the use of gas itself, but Finkel's failure to explain that its use would be limited, which would have required him to simply indicate the volume of gas he believes will be required – a failure repeated in this essay.

Finkel argues that "natural gas will be a part of Australia's energy mix for many years to come" because of its important role in providing "firming" for renewable generators. There is wide support for this position from, among other respected sources, the Integrated System Plan prepared by the Australian Energy Market Operator (AEMO) and, most recently, a Grattan Institute report (an earlier Grattan report is highly critical of the government's "gas-led recovery" proposals). However, both AEMO and Grattan say that the volume of gas required will be very small and will certainly not require any increase in gas-fired generation capacity. In all of the scenarios modelled by AEMO for the Integrated System Plan, the share of gas generation in total electricity supply will be significantly lower than its current level, which is already low (about 5 per cent per year in the National Electricity Market). By failing to state that the share of gas generation needed will be small and transitional, or to reference the AEMO plan, Finkel (perhaps inadvertently) allows his words to be used by the government to advocate building new gas-fired power stations and increasing, rather than decreasing, the share of gas generation.

This may seem a rather nitpicking criticism, but the key point is that Australia, and almost all other countries, have already delayed acting decisively to reduce emissions for far too long. We cannot afford to make any investments, such as new gas-fuelled generators, which will lock emissions at higher than absolutely necessary levels for years to come.

When I reached the end of the essay, having read what Finkel himself calls a "gloomy forecast" in the section on climate change, the very last words came as a shock: "be patient." The rationale for this injunction is the time it will take for the new energy-supply technologies, most especially hydrogen, to reach technological maturity. But this argument reflects that the essay is largely written from the supply-side perspective, as it is called in energy policy terminology. While only some forms of energy are sources of greenhouse gases, those gases are only emitted to the atmosphere when that energy is used, in relevant types of equipment, to deliver energy services for consumers. The energy system consists not only of energy-supply technologies and equipment, which are where fossil carbon originates, but also energy-using technologies and equipment, from which fossil carbon is emitted as fossil carbon dioxide. Energy-using or demand-side technologies are no less important, though less exciting, than supply-side technologies, when thinking about energy-system transition. The energy used to deliver transport and thermal processes (heat) is currently supplied almost entirely by petroleum products, gas and coal, and it accounts for about half of Australia's total energy combustion emissions. Replacing these fuels with electricity and hydrogen means completely replacing existing equipment with new equipment that uses electricity and hydrogen.

As Finkel explains, transitioning the energy supply to renewable electricity and hydrogen will require investments of many billions of dollars, but the investment decisions themselves will be made by a relatively small cohort of executives – certainly far fewer than a million, if passive corporate shareholders are excluded. By contrast, there are over 4 million householders and small-business owners with gas connections to their dwellings or business premises, almost all of whom use gas for space heating, water heating or both. Gas heaters typically have an operational life of at least twenty years. How long will it take to replace them all with reverse-cycle air conditioners and heat-pump or electric-resistance water heaters (often a sensible choice for buildings with rooftop solar generation)?

Unless decisive action to drive the changeover is introduced very soon, state governments will be unable to meet their net-zero emissions targets by 2050, except by mandating the scrapping and replacement of serviceable gas appliances and providing appropriate compensation to hundreds of thousands – or millions – of appliance owners. We cannot afford to be patient about starting this transition.

Nor can we be patient about road transport emissions. The number of registered passenger and light commercial motor vehicles in 2020 was about 18 million, according to ABS statistics. The number of individual owners is not known, but is likely to be over 10 million. New vehicle sales each year are equal to about 7 per cent of the total registered fleet, and the average age of registered passenger and light commercial vehicles is about ten years. It is certainly the case that older vehicles travel less distance than newer ones; in 2019–20, vehicles that were fifteen or more years old accounted for about 26 per cent of registered vehicles but only 17 per cent of the total distance travelled. Nevertheless, unless far more aggressive policies to support the uptake of electric vehicles are introduced in the near future, a target of zero-emissions road transport by 2050 will be unattainable.

It is obvious that the issues I have raised combine technology with policy, and that is why the attempt to separate the two creates problems. I suspect that Finkel may share my view that announcing emission-reduction targets without providing some details of the policy program by which the target will be achieved is like announcing an aspiration or a hope and is actually quite useless as a way of "getting to zero." However, a carefully compiled and skilfully written menu of new technologies is also useless by itself, irrespective of how much more attractive the new technologies may be than old emissions-intensive technologies, on the basis of either performance or cost. The menu must be accompanied by an account of how the technologies will be rolled out on the scale needed to get to zero. The perceived need to separate "technology" from "policy" seems to be yet another manifestation of how the poisonous politics surrounding the climate change challenge in Australia continue to impede real progress on planning for deep emissions reduction.

Hugh Saddler

GETTING
TO ZERO

Correspondence

Ketan Joshi

Alan Finkel closes the introduction of his recent Quarterly Essay with a quote from the Borg, a fictitious species from *Star Trek: The Next Generation*: "resistance is futile." Finkel's plea: stop "cave dwelling" and accept the unavoidable technological carbon revolution.

The Borg are not meant to be inspirational: they are cybernetic life forms, assimilating individuals from other species into "drones." They are an emotionless hive, obsessed with technology and with no care for individuality, emotion, passion or morals. Finkel does not quote the Borg's chilling declaration in full: "We will add your biological and technological distinctiveness to our own. Your culture will adapt to service us. Resistance is futile." Like so much science fiction, the Borg represent a real-world threat – technology for technology's sake, single-minded and cold, with culture, community and the welfare of life left out of the equation.

While technology is a necessary component of climate action, it is insufficient. Fossil fuels have sunk deep into our way of life, and removing them as fast as possible will require significant political, cultural and corporate shifts. Climate action must be restorative and curative, imbued with justice and fairness and the righting of wrongs, so that it is demanded, rather than merely tolerated, by people.

And it must be fast: every day wasted sees more megatons of greenhouse gases produced, and consequently, more heating of Earth's habitats. The quantity of greenhouse gases our species can release before we know for sure the planet will overshoot 1.5°C of warming is now vanishingly small, thanks to decades of delay. That means moving as fast as possible is the only response.

The "possible" in "fast as possible" changes depending whom you ask. If you ask Australia's government, anything faster than dangerously slow is unthinkable heresy. At the time of writing, the prime minister cannot even commit to net zero by 2050, a basic step most countries took some time ago. Targets, carbon budgets, short-term plans and ambitious policy are not only non-existent but publicly derided.

On Network Ten's *The Project* in September 2020, Finkel was pressed on the urgency and highlighted the wording of the Paris Agreement, in which signatories must achieve net-zero emissions "within the second half of this century."

He said: "It could be 2099. It's important that people don't feel there's only one way to achieve an ambition. There could be multiple ways."

This is not accurate. The longer the delay, the more emissions and the worse the climate impacts. Wealthy, emissions-intensive countries are bound by the Paris Agreement's equity considerations to put their backs into this. Australia has historically emitted far more than its fair share, and should therefore cut emissions more steeply than countries in the Global South. That means reaching net zero well *before* 2050.

The approach adopted by Finkel and by the Australian government – "we'll get there when we get there" – has already had dire consequences. The latest projections show that with existing policies, Australia's emissions will be around 22 per cent below their 2005 levels in 2030 – well above the 26 per cent Paris target, even accounting for the growth in renewables. Australia needs a reduction of between 66 per cent and 80 per cent on 2005 levels by 2030, and net zero between 2035 and 2045, to support a global 1.5°C climate target.

That means a full phase-out of coal power before 2030 and all fossil fuels before 2035. That means aggressive government policy to incentivise zero-carbon transport (public transport, cycling, walking and electric vehicles) along with dates for combustion-engine sales bans. That means a plan to phase out fossil fuels from heating and industry over the next two decades. That means a safety net for every fossil-fuel worker. Australia is a full-scale failure on every single point. In short, it means rapid, immediate action, rather than a plea to sit back and wait for a contrived technological deus ex machina in the final act of this half-century.

Australia could have been comfortably on the pathway to 1.5°C-aligned emissions cuts if the government had begun when the Paris Agreement was signed. In that case, cuts of around 21 megatons of carbon dioxide equivalent (MtCO2-e) each year would be required. In 2020, that is now 30 MtCO2-e. With another five years of delay, it'll be 47 MtCO2-e. The government's most recent projections predict an annual fall of between 1 and 6 MtCO2-e per year before 2030. Why don't these numbers feature in Finkel's essay?

A laid back, non-interventionist "tech'll fix it" approach dooms Australia to a significantly slower transition, and significantly worse emissions, alongside the continued enrichment of the fossil-fuel industry. It is a vision of false comfort and real climate impacts. Those emissions will hurt human beings and erode the natural world. Resistance is not futile – it is everywhere, and it is dangerous.

Finkel's essay is at its best when it is outlining the history of fossil fuels, or explaining the fascinating science behind climate solutions. It is at its worst – and most consequential – when it works to justify the slow, incremental and dangerous approach to the climate threat being deployed by Australia's government. To treat climate as a crisis is decried as "perfectionism," and the only calm, level-headed approach is to go with the free-market technological flow.

Part of this go-slow approach manifests as a desire to ensure climate action is undetectable – something that requires no change to Australian life. Big, comfortable, energy-intensive and inefficient, the classic Australian lifestyle can stay that way even as Australia's energy system is swapped out with "low-carbon" alternatives. The change is purely under the hood (in some sectors, literally).

Part of this logic stems from the false assumption that climate deniers abound in society and would be alienated by aggressive climate action. "Thus, even those who are not convinced about the threat posed by climate change should be enthusiastic about the transformations that are underway," said Finkel.

This was best illustrated in an interview with the *7am* podcast, in which Finkel said, "I don't think that the alternatives to changing our lifestyles, such as global population control or behavioural change so that we all ride bicycles instead of cars, are likely," and even went so far as to assert that active transport like cycling doesn't make a "substantial difference" to emissions.

Aside from being demonstrably untrue, it's a cop-out. "Behavioural change" is treated like a millstone around the neck, whereas in its best manifestation it is an empowering tool for citizen participation. Finkel rightly dismisses ecofascist appeals to depopulation, but wrongly dismisses cultural change as risky and unacceptable. It is a cold, unambitious view that excludes the possibility that Australians might actually prefer to be participants in the greatest transformation in history. And when discussing decarbonising aviation, for instance, he doesn't mention the simple possibility of flying less – either through cutting down on business travel, or by means of remote meetings and land-based electric transport.

Around the world, it has become startlingly clear that the fastest way to decarbonise transport (and most other sectors) is through a suite of changes that consider environmental justice, racism and class disparities. Greater access to public transport, active transport and electrified vehicles work in unison, enabled through activism, effort, politics and community. Social and cultural lifestyle change can feed into personal divestment from fossil fuels, and political and corporate pressure. This parody of rapid climate harm reduction as "sacrifice and loss" is outdated and irrelevant, now serving only as a rhetorical tool to protect declining revenues for the fossil-fuel industry.

At the core of Finkel's essay is the argument that a fast transition is impossible. It's common for techno-optimists to be wildly pessimistic about massive, rapid social change. Finkel repeats a trope used frequently by the fossil-fuel industry: "we can't shut off fossil fuels overnight." Somehow, the fact that a 100 per cent cut in emissions can't be made in twelve hours proves the impossibility of a reasonably fast transition – such as one aligned with a 1.5°C target over the next ten to twenty years. Of course it is possible – if we go beyond metal and money, and consider activism, effort and cultural change, along with massive political efforts to phase out fossil-fuel burning and extraction swiftly.

The frequently repeated warning of the danger of reducing emissions too fast echoes big climate names, such as Bill Gates and Vaclav Smil, who likely inspire Finkel's claim that "the notion that we can suddenly reverse the slope of emissions is implausible." Of course, Australia is far from being anywhere close to altering that slope. At the current rate of reduction projected between 2020 and 2030, Australia will fall to zero emissions somewhere around 2294. But nobody said this would be easy, and if we're dismissing effortful action then we're permanently doomed.

Another key justification for reducing emissions far slower than possible is an appeal to "technology neutrality." It's meant to signify a calm, level-headed and *very serious* objectivity; a capability to assess machines on their engineering and scientific merits, and to remain unclouded by the emotions of activists and environmentalists. Finkel laments being asked to reduce emissions quickly without nuclear, fossil hydrogen and carbon capture: a "litany of proscribed approaches."

Finkel is proud of being "the only genuinely technology-neutral person in the room." But climate centrism is toxic, because it presupposes that a single view of what is "feasible" is the logical, adult and final one, rather than something which shifts over time and is subject to democratic and social processes.

In practice, what this means is ignorance of how the promise of future technology is used by fossil-fuel companies and politicians as a reason to delay. Carbon capture and storage (CCS) is the perfect example; "clean coal" and CCS have been promised as the saviours of climate for decades. "There is no reason why by 2020 we can't be putting a quarter of our emissions from coal and gas back into the ground, and no reason why by 2030 it wouldn't be about half," said chief executive of the Australian Coal Association (now the Minerals Council) Mark O'Neill in *The Australian* in 2006.

In 2019, Australia released around 411 megatons of fossil carbon dioxide emissions. About 3 megatons were captured that year in Western Australia's Gorgon facility. For the same year, the world released 36,440 megatons of fossil-origin carbon dioxide. The total carbon capture capacity in that year was 40 megatons, most dedicated to "enhanced oil recovery," in which captured carbon is used to extract and sell more oil. No, that is not a quarter. It's 0.1 per cent. What's the "neutral" verdict on that?

In Victoria, a plan to produce hydrogen using the state's massive reserves of coal – among the most climate-damaging on Earth – comes bundled with a pinky promise to implement a carbon capture system nearly double that of Australia's existing capacity (by my calculations). This promise, the Victorian government's "CarbonNet" carbon storage project, is more than a decade old now, and isn't likely to capture a single molecule any time in the coming years. "Start-up is planned for between 2015 and 2019," wrote Norwegian energy technology site Zero, in 2012. We know the service CCS provides. It is a rhetorical and political service, not a technological one.

Finkel shrugs off the hazards of CCS false promises by declaring that no market will exist for high-emissions hydrogen. That is dangerously naive. Right now, the world's fossil-gas producers are engaging in a massive marketing campaign to promote "carbon-neutral LNG," the same old fossil fuels paired with highly suspect carbon offset schemes. Finkel is badly underestimating how good the fossil-fuel industry is at obfuscation, public relations and regulatory capture.

There will be a massive market for high-emissions fossil hydrogen, and it will be realised through the existing global machine of marketing and deception used by fossil-fuel companies to stave off their demise by decades. Ditto for a hydrogen climate impact "certification scheme," something almost certain to bow to fossil industry pressure and become a massive global greenwashing project.

Finkel's support for gas in Australia's energy system – both as a fuel for home heating and cooking and grid-level "emergency" backup – shows a similar naivety. The gas industry will happily and successfully go far beyond providing a few hours of emergency backup – the current government is planning to build a 660-megawatt fossil-gas plant in New South Wales, despite the grid operator insisting it is absolutely not needed for grid reliability.

Of course, the government has also literally called its COVID-19 response package a "gas-fired recovery." Will companies start aggressively blending hydrogen into the pipelines feeding fossil gas into Australian homes, or will they decarbonise in literally microscopic increments over decades, while pleading they're acting on climate? The fossil-gas industry is already publishing studies attacking electrification and promoting pathways that protect the value of pipelines and processing plants, despite those pathways resulting in far greater cumulative emissions due to going slower.

Climate centrism serves the fossil-fuel industry. "Technology neutrality" creates a playground for fossil companies to maximise profits at the cost of direct harm to human life. In Finkel's essay, anything outside the middle of the road is "perfectionism" or climate denial, and both are dismissed accordingly. In reality, the planet will continue to warm for as long as net greenhouse gas emissions are greater than zero, and any plea to go slower than as fast as possible comes packaged with an implicit acceptance of worsening climate harm.

Finkel's essay ends by painting a picture of a net-zero world that is essentially the same as today's, sans greenhouse gas molecules. Australia is wealthy, comfortable and energy-intensive. But there is no due date for this vision, creating room for a go-slow on climate action – breathing room for the fossil-fuel industry at the cost of public health and safety.

It is a dangerous thing to present climate action as inevitable. It is the speed of climate action that determines how much harm we will experience – the debate on whether to act has come and gone. Delay is the main game for fossil industries now, enacted through the rhetoric of false technological promises and greenwashed climate plans.

As the summer of 2020 showed, Australia will experience the consequences of delay directly. A gentle slope to reduce emissions may have been possible in the 1990s, but the hour is now late. There are only two choices: bloated delay and worsened climate impacts, or rapid action and lesser climate impacts. Our efforts now should go towards figuring out how to ensure that rapid action is fair, fast and furious.

It is demonstrably untrue that "resistance is futile." Australia's fossil-fuel industry has manufactured a situation in which there is a broad political, social and cultural blindness to the nerve-racking urgency of emissions reductions. Resistance to climate action is everywhere – Australia is drowning in it, and burning and boiling too. Decarbonisation is indeed inevitable. But empty technological promises, a hostility towards hard climate targets and a refusal to take any short-term action mean the decline of the fossil-fuel industry is so shallow that it's essentially a straight line. Resistance is profitable, and that is the problem Australia's former chief scientist ought to be addressing.

Ketan Joshi

GETTING TO ZERO

Correspondence

Ian Lowe

Dr Finkel correctly warns of the complexity and formidable challenges involved in achieving the target of zero emissions. As a former chief scientist, he is understandably reluctant to comment on the political climate and the extent to which elected politicians represent an obstacle to progress, but we must be realistic. While better technologies are more likely to succeed, we don't live in a world of technological determinism. Policy decisions by governments have a critical impact on the scale and rate of progress.

There are some technical issues on which I believe the essay is unhelpfully optimistic. It is not sensible to talk about "zero-emissions" nuclear energy. It would be equally misleading to talk about "zero-emissions" solar or wind energy. In each of those cases, carbon-based fuels are not burned to produce the delivered electricity, but significant amounts of emissions are required to fabricate solar panels, wind turbines and nuclear power stations. Overall, they produce much less emissions than burning fossil fuels, but they are not zero-emissions technologies. That label implies we can cheerfully scale them up to meet any improbable level of demand.

The essay also refers to "carbon capture and permanent storage." The promise of CCS has been used repeatedly as a get-out-of-jail-free card by those who want to keep using fossil fuels. Don't worry, they argue, the carbon will be captured and permanently stored. There are three problems. First, it has not been convincingly demonstrated that carbon dioxide, liquefied and injected into geological layers, will stay there forever. Secondly, the process of capturing and liquefying carbon dioxide uses considerable quantities of energy (and costs a lot of money). Thirdly, while there may be some niche operations that use this technology because there are suitable strata near the site producing the carbon dioxide, it is simply not credible to envisage it being scaled up to manage the global problem. The volume of carbon dioxide that would be produced if we captured and liquefied the gas from the world's coal-fired power stations would be comparable with that handled by the world's entire oil industry. That volume would need to be transported and stored in suitable geological strata every year. It just can't happen.

On the other hand, I think the essay understates the pace of change in the global electricity industry. After noting that solar and wind accounted for almost all new generating capacity in recent years in Australia, it states, "In the rest of the world, the comparable figure is a bit over half, because natural gas and coal-fired generators continue to be built." In 2019, the world installed about 170 gigawatts of new renewables and about 70 gigawatts of fossil-fuel generators. So "the comparable figure" wasn't "a bit over half" but about 70 per cent. The International Energy Agency's 2020 figures are even stronger: 107 gigawatts of solar, 65 gigawatts of wind and 18 gigawatts of hydro, giving a total of 190 gigawatts of new renewable capacity. New gas? About 40 gigawatts. Coal? Zero. In fact, the closures slightly exceeded new capacity, making 2020 the first year in living memory in which coal capacity declined. So last year, renewables were over 80 per cent of new capacity globally. What about nuclear power? IEA estimated 8 gigawatts of new capacity coming on line but 5 gigawatts being decommissioned, giving a net gain of 3 gigawatts, compared with 190 gigawatts of renewables. It is clear which way the world as a whole is going.

The editor of the annual World Nuclear Industry Status Report, Mycle Schneider, recently gave figures for the changes in the average prices of power from different supply sources in the last decade. Coal-fired electricity went up slightly, from 11.1 to 11.2 cents per kilowatt-hour, while nuclear power increased from 12.3 cents to 16.3. By contrast, the average price of wind power came down from 13.5 cents to 4.0, while solar improved from 35.9 cents a decade ago to an average of 3.7 cents a kilowatt-hour in 2020, with one new installation in Portugal delivering energy for 1.1 cents. That change in the economics is breathtaking. Ten years ago, solar power cost about three times as much as nuclear power, on average, while wind was slightly more expensive than nuclear. Now, nuclear power is more than four times the average price of either solar or wind power.

The economics is driving change in the way existing capacity is being used. The International Energy Agency's figures for the absolute changes in delivered electricity between 2019 and 2020 are startling: renewables about 400 terawatt-hours more, coal about 500 terawatt-hours less, gas about 130 terawatt-hours less, nuclear about 100 terawatt-hours less.

I was disappointed by the essay's lack of emphasis on the need to improve the efficiency of using energy. There is a statement that says it all: "If our use of energy were more efficient, we would not have to produce nearly as much." Quite. People don't want energy, they want hot showers, cold beer and the ability to get around. But the discussion of supply needs implicitly assumes we will continue to waste massive amounts of energy through inefficiency. The National Framework for Energy Efficiency, presented to the Howard government in 2003, estimated we could reduce our emissions by 30 per cent using cost-effective existing technology, with payback times of less than four years. Almost nothing has been done in the eighteen years since to implement these recommendations, or to utilise the subsequent improvements in technology. Our electrical appliances, our vehicles and our buildings are very inefficient, wasting money as well as energy. Solar hot water makes economic sense almost everywhere but is still not encouraged by the national government. Rather than introducing efficiency standards to entice motorists to buy smaller vehicles, we have encouraged the move to large SUVs, while the retreat from sensible urban planning and the lack of public transport has condemned thousands of people living on the edges of our cities to long commutes by car. We could live at the same level of material comfort using half the energy we now do. That would make more sense than continuing to invest in ever-increasing amounts of supply.

Dr Finkel's optimistic closing vision of a net-zero-emissions future is one I would dearly like to see. We should be moving urgently in that direction. But we need to be realistic – and angry – about the formidable obstacle that is the bitterly divided Coalition government. I recently talked with farmers who were apoplectic about the National Party's failure to recognise the damage climate change is doing to rural Australia. "Haven't they noticed we are having one-in-a-hundred-year events every bloody year?" one said. Apart from stupidly waving a lump of coal around in parliament before he displaced Malcolm Turnbull, Scott Morrison has restricted himself to baseless claims that we will meet "in a canter" our inadequate Paris target. Josh Frydenberg, while Turnbull's energy and environment minister, attacked South Australia's Weatherill government for investing in solar, wind and battery storage. It was a nakedly political attack; there has been no criticism of South Australia's current Coalition government for doubling down on that successful strategy since it was elected. While the modest carbon price set by the Gillard government clearly reduced emissions, it was demonised by the Coalition as a great big tax on everything, with ridiculous claims it would make a lamb roast cost $100 and reduce Whyalla to a ghost town. Everyone from right-wing economists to leftish environmentalists would support a price on greenhouse gas emissions, but that is ruled out on ideological grounds. The election of Zali Steggall and the recent support of her climate initiative by other crossbenchers should be a warning to the government. Once the dust has settled from the pandemic and the toxic patriarchal culture in Parliament House, the big challenge for our politics will be responding to climate change. Tony Abbott will not be the last casualty if the government continues to be part of the problem, rather than part of the solution.

Ian Lowe

GETTING TO ZERO

Response to Correspondence

Alan Finkel

There is such a broad and overlapping range of views in the commentaries that it seems sensible to respond in categories.

Natural gas in electricity generation

The important role of gas-fired electricity in supporting rapid deployment of solar and wind continues to be underappreciated. The key issue is that electricity is an essential service, and interruptions of supply have huge economic, personal and political ramifications. There is no other commodity for which supply interruptions in the vicinity of seconds and minutes are even noticed, let alone damaging. Electricity is unique.

As coal-fired generators retire, we must build solar and wind electricity generators to compensate. However, solar and wind electricity sources are variable, and without alternative storage or generation to back them up – a process known as "firming" – the electricity system will be unreliable.

Batteries will increasingly contribute to the firming role, but we need enough of them, and we need to set aside some of the solar and wind electricity to charge them. Batteries are getting cheaper and more plentiful, but it is not clear that we could deploy them at the rate that will be needed if coal-fired generators continue to close down earlier than anticipated.

Natural gas-fired generators are already in the system. They can provide the firming that is needed. They have the added benefit over batteries that they can run not only for minutes and hours but for days and weeks. These long-duration needs are real: there are occasions in winter where the wind can average less than 10 per cent of normal for a week at a time.

The key question is, do we need *new* gas-fired generators? The answer depends on two important considerations: distribution and peak power.

On distribution, the challenge is to have the firming generators where they are needed. The transmission grid is not sufficiently dense to support perfect utilisation of any given generator across the National Electricity Market, which stretches 5000 kilometres from Port Douglas in Queensland to Port Lincoln in South Australia.[1] And for cost and local environmental impact reasons, it never will be. Therefore, generators need to be spread out and occasionally new ones might be needed to fill gaps.

On peak power, even if the natural gas generators do not get used much during the year, when they are called upon to meet peak demand you might need them all. That is, if there is a week-long lull in wind during the winter months across a large state that needs to meet a peak power shortfall of 5 gigawatts, if natural gas generation is called upon we need 5 gigawatts worth of generators all running at the same time.

Put differently, a single generator that on average operates 4000 hours per year is not nearly as useful as ten generators that on average operate 400 hours per year. It may be, as Hugh Saddler says, that the total volume of gas required for electricity generation across the system might not increase, but as coal-fired generators close down, we will occasionally need more gas generators operating simultaneously, infrequently, to ensure that we can meet the instantaneous peak demands of the system.

Another consideration is that coal-fired generators typically operate for 5000 hours per year, whereas a gas generator used for firming will typically operate fewer than 500 hours per year. And each of those hours produces electricity at a significantly lower emissions level than electricity from coal-fired generators. Thus, the emissions from a gas-fired generator used for firming are very small, even if the nameplate capacity in megawatts is quite high.

Take the most recent example, the gas generator to be built at Kurri Kuri in the Hunter Valley. It is expected to operate 2 per cent of the time, or 175 hours per year.[2] This is a tiny fraction of the soon to-be-closed Liddell coal-fired power station 80 kilometres away, which during the last five years operated an average of 52 per cent of the time, or about 4550 hours per year.[3] And the Kurri Kurri generator only has about a third of the output power of the Liddell station. All up, its annual generation is miniscule in comparison to that of the Liddell coal plant, but its role to support the solar and wind electricity that will replace the bulk of the output from Liddell will occasionally be crucially important.

In summary, the Kurri Kurri gas-fired generator is in no conceivable way intended to replace the output from the Liddell coal-fired station. Instead, it will firm up solar and wind to prevent blackouts and higher prices after the power station closes at the end of the summer in 2023.

The International Energy Agency (IEA) has been quoted as saying that no new natural gas generators should be built. That is not correct. What the IEA said is that there is no need for new oil and gas fields to be developed in its net-zero model.[4] Also, and perhaps surprisingly, the IEA model shows natural gas generation increasing for the next five years, with a decline after that. This is consistent with a shift towards natural gas generation playing more of a firming role and less of a replacement role.[5] Whether or not new natural gas generators should be built is a different question, the answer to which depends both on how fast coal-fired generators retire and on our ability to meet peak demand. The faster that coal-fired generators retire, the more we might need to call on natural gas generators to firm the solar and wind electricity that replaces the coal generation.

And yes, if new generators are built, they should certainly be installed with the intention of eventually running them on hydrogen, initially blended in at low percentages, but eventually operating on 100 per cent hydrogen.

Hydrogen

Around the world, not just in Australia, forward-looking countries such as Germany, France, the United Kingdom and Japan are looking to develop hydrogen as a clean fuel alternative to coal, oil and natural gas. Not in all applications – electricity from solar, wind and hydroelectricity will be the main replacement fuel – but hydrogen will be used in those applications where a high-density energy carrier is required, and in some cases where an alternative industrial chemical feedstock is required. Richie Merzian says that in the briefing called *Hydrogen for Australia's Future*, my colleagues and I overstated that potential. To the contrary, the growing interest since then indicates that we were conservative. Through the lens of his personal experience, Ben Wilson confirms the potential for hydrogen to help us decarbonise our building heating and hot water energy needs by replacing natural gas in our distribution system with hydrogen. Just two months after my Quarterly Essay was published, Ben's company welcomed the future when it flicked the switch to connect 700 houses in Adelaide to a 5 per cent hydrogen blend in their gas supply.

The vast majority of clean hydrogen will be produced by using renewable electricity to crack water, but some in future might be produced using fossil fuels with carbon capture and permanent storage (CCS). Whether or not that occurs will depend on economics. The hydrogen so produced will be subject to a certification process to verify the emissions. Hydrogen produced by electrolysis will be subject to the same certification process. CCS for a zero-emissions future is strongly supported by the Intergovernmental Panel on Climate Change (IPCC), the IEA and the Biden administration.[6]

Equity

The key reason for reducing emissions to net zero is fairness to current and future generations. For fairness, the transition to a net-zero energy system must also ensure that the cost of the future energy supply is low and that the supply is available to all. In my essay, I argued that the way to achieve this is through driving the cost of new and emerging low-emissions technologies down to the tipping point at which they become cheaper than the high-emissions incumbent technologies. Cheap, clean, reliable energy will not emerge from a focus on "environmental justice, racism and class disparities," as argued by Ketan Joshi. Instead, these important equity outcomes will be supported by the efficient delivery of the technological change.

Scott Ludlam makes the point that rather than maintaining our energy-profligate society, we should choose a path of lower impact and take into consideration land rights, regenerative economics and circular design principles. Equivalently, Ian Lowe quite rightly points to the need to improve the efficiency with which we use energy. Yes, we should, and it is important to have policies in place to encourage high-efficiency technologies and practices. Uptake of these high-efficiency solutions by the majority of the population will then depend on personal economics and policy guidance from social scientists.

Science and policy

The scientific evidence for global warming and climate change is overwhelming. I am glad that most commentators acknowledged the strength of my description of the fundamentals. The question then becomes the role, not the fact, of the scientific evidence.

No one point of view will ever, realistically, determine political and even practical outcomes. The coronavirus pandemic provides an example. We saw in Australia that health and scientific advice was taken into account by authorities to an unprecedented degree. The Rapid Research Information Forum that I convened and chaired provided up-to-the-minute expert advice to ministers, and of course the state, territory and federal chief medical officers had the dominant advisory role. And they were listened to, by the prime minister, premiers, first ministers and health ministers, and by the public. But if decisions had been made solely on the basis of the health advice, we would have faced an economic disaster. Instead, the government leaders also listened to the advice of state, territory and federal treasuries and other economic experts. The net health and economic outcome in Australia was among the best in the world.

Similarly, when it comes to responding to the threat of climate change, we have to listen to the scientists. But we also have to listen to the economists, and the engineers who operate our energy networks, and the farmers and industrial workers. We need to reduce emissions as rapidly as possible while ensuring ongoing economic prosperity. To choose one need over the other would be irresponsible. As Boris Johnson said at Biden's Leaders Summit on Climate in April, the goal is "cake, have, eat."[7]

When Tim Flannery makes the argument that we have to shut down coal-fired generation immediately because the science says so, this ambition has to be reconciled with the reality that more than 60 per cent of our electricity generation comes from coal. Shutting it down immediately is not an option. Instead, we have to make coal-fired electricity obsolete by replacing it with a clean, firm, cheap and abundant alternative. This alternative will be a complex mixture of solar, wind, batteries, software, long-distance transmission lines, responsive loads, overbuilding of solar and wind generation, and in some cases infrequently used natural gas generation.

Yes, as Rebecca Huntley says, we need policy to drive technological change. That policy is constantly evolving and under challenge. My goal in writing the Quarterly Essay was to show that technology can deliver if policy is supportive. I agree with Nick Rowley that technology does not live in a policy vacuum, but for the reasons he outlines in his commentary, I believe that I can maximise my effectiveness as an adviser on getting to zero by focusing on the key technologies that will make it possible.

Ross Garnaut raises the importance of reducing methane emissions. I couldn't agree more, and I am overjoyed that scientific research is delivering potential solutions to the enteric fermentation in cattle and sheep that globally contributes most of the methane emissions. There are also technologies that can be applied to reduce fugitive emissions, but the best way to eliminate fugitive emissions is to replace oil, coal and gas with renewable alternatives.

Garnaut (in passing) and Ian McAuley (in detail) mention the role that a carbon tax can have in driving the exit from high-emissions technologies. Whether a carbon tax is referred to as a tax, a price or a trading scheme, it has complex consequences beyond driving the exit from high-emissions technologies. For me to have entered that debate in my Quarterly Essay would have undermined my ability to convey my main message, which is that through investing in new and emerging zero-emissions technologies we can build the scale that will enable newcomers to match the price of the high-emissions incumbents, at which point we will benefit from a tipping point and all rational users will purchase the zero-emissions alternative.

Bill Gates describes this strategy as eliminating the "Green Premium."[8] Early adopters are happy to pay a Green Premium, but the majority of the population will not. The ultimate goal that I aspire to is to convert the cost disparity into a "Green Discount."

Alan Finkel

1 Australian Energy Market Commission, "National Electricity Market", AEMC website, www.aemc.gov.au/energy-system/electricity/electricity-system/NEM, accessed 1 June 2021.

2 Jacobs Group, "Hunter Power Project: Environmental Impact Statement", report, 22 April 2021.

3 Wikipedia, "Liddell Power Station", 24 March 2021, https://en.wikipedia.org/wiki/Liddell_Power_Station.

4 International Energy Agency, "Net Zero by 2050: A Roadmap for the Global Energy Sector", special report, May 2021, https://iea.blob.core.windows.net/assets/ad0d4830-bd7e-47b6-838c-40d115733c13/NetZeroby2050-ARoadmapfortheGlobalEnergySector.pdf.

5 *Ibid.*

6 Daniel Gros, "The Green Art of the Possible", *The Business Times*, 7 May 2021.

7 Fiona Harvey, "Boris Johnson Urges Leaders to 'Get Serious' at Climate Summit", *The Guardian*, 23 April 2021.

8 Bill Gates introduced the term "Green Premium" in his book *How to Avoid a Climate Disaster*.

Alan Finkel was Australia's chief scientist from 2016 to 2020. He is a neuroscientist, engineer and entrepreneur. He led the 2017 National Electricity Market Review and the 2019 development of the National Hydrogen Strategy, and chaired the 2020 panel developing the Low Emissions Technology Roadmap. He is currently special adviser to the Australian government on low-emissions technologies.

Tim Flannery is the author of more than a dozen books, including *The Future Eaters*, *Throwim Way Leg*, *The Weather Makers*, *Now or Never*, *Here on Earth* and *The Climate Cure*. In 2007 he was the Australian of the Year.

Ross Garnaut is the professorial research fellow in economics at the University of Melbourne. In 2008, he produced the Garnaut Climate Change Review for the federal, state and territory governments of Australia. He is the author of many books, including the bestselling *The Great Crash of 2008*, *Dog Days*, *Superpower* and *Reset*.

Rebecca Huntley is one of Australia's leading social researchers. She was formerly the director of the Mind & Mood Report, Australia's longest-running social trends report, and led Vox Populi research. Her books include *Still Lucky*, *Australia Fair* and *How to Talk about Climate Change in a Way That Makes a Difference*.

Ketan Joshi is a writer, analyst and consultant working on climate and energy. He is based in Oslo and is the author of *Windfall: Unlocking a Fossil-Free Future*.

Ian Lowe is an emeritus professor of science, technology and society at Griffith University and was a reviewer for the United Nations–sponsored 2005 Millennium Assessment Report and the 2004 report of the International Geosphere-Biosphere Program. His books include *Living in the Hothouse*, *A Big Fix* and the Quarterly Essay *Reaction Time*.

Scott Ludlam is an ICAN ambassador and a former Australian Greens senator for Western Australia. He is the author of *Full Circle: A Search for the World That Comes Next*.

Ian McAuley is a fellow of the Centre for Policy Development. He was formerly a lecturer in public finance at the University of Canberra and is now retired. In his earliest professional career, he was a power systems engineer.

George Megalogenis has thirty years' experience in the media, including over a decade in the federal parliamentary press gallery. His book *The Australian Moment* won the 2013 Prime Minister's Literary Award for non-fiction and the 2012 Walkley Book Award, and formed the basis for the ABC documentary series *Making Australia Great*. His most recent book is *The Football Solution* and he is also author of *Australia's Second Chance, The Longest Decade, Faultlines* and two previous Quarterly Essays, *Trivial Pursuit and Balancing Act*.

Richie Merzian is the inaugural director of the Climate & Energy Program at independent think-tank the Australia Institute. Formerly, he was Australia's lead negotiator on adaptation to the UN Framework Convention on Climate Change. He worked in the Department of Climate Change and the Department of Foreign Affairs on domestic and international climate and energy agendas for almost a decade.

Nick Rowley has worked on addressing climate change for more than twenty years: first as an adviser to NSW premier Bob Carr and then working directly with UK prime minister Tony Blair for two years at 10 Downing Street. He has also taught in the Master of Public Policy program at the University of Sydney.

Hugh Saddler is an honorary associate professor at the Crawford School of Public Policy, Australian National University. He has worked as an academic and consultant, researching and writing about energy and climate-change policy, since the time of the oil shocks in the 1970s.

Ben Wilson is the CEO of the Australian Gas Infrastructure Group, one of Australia's largest utilities. He has been in energy for twenty-five years – in banking and then in UK electricity distribution.

20 YEARS OF QUARTERLY ESSAY

Subscribe to the Friends of Quarterly Essay email newsletter to share in news, updates, events and special offers as we celebrate our 20th anniversary.

quarterlyessay.com.au/signup

QUARTERLY ESSAY
BACK ISSUES

BACK ISSUES: (Prices include GST, postage and handling within Australia.) *Grey indicates out of stock.*

- ☐ **QE 1** ($17.99) Robert Manne *In Denial*
- ☐ **QE 2** ($17.99) John Birmingham *Appeasing Jakarta*
- ☐ **QE 3** ($17.99) Guy Rundle *The Opportunist*
- ☐ **QE 4** ($17.99) Don Watson *Rabbit Syndrome*
- ☐ **QE 5** ($17.99) Mungo MacCallum *Girt By Sea*
- ☐ **QE 6** ($17.99) John Button *Beyond Belief*
- ☐ **QE 7** ($17.99) John Martinkus *Paradise Betrayed*
- ☐ **QE 8** ($17.99) Amanda Lohrey *Groundswell*
- ☐ **QE 9** ($17.99) Tim Flannery *Beautiful Lies*
- ☐ **QE 10** ($17.99) Gideon Haigh *Bad Company*
- ☐ **QE 11** ($17.99) Germaine Greer *Whitefella Jump Up*
- ☐ **QE 12** ($17.99) David Malouf *Made in England*
- ☐ **QE 13** ($17.99) Robert Manne with David Corlett *Sending Them Home*
- ☐ **QE 14** ($17.99) Paul McGeough *Mission Impossible*
- ☐ **QE 15** ($17.99) Margaret Simons *Latham's World*
- ☐ **QE 16** ($17.99) Raimond Gaita *Breach of Trust*
- ☐ **QE 17** ($17.99) John Hirst *'Kangaroo Court'*
- ☐ **QE 18** ($17.99) Gail Bell *The Worried Well*
- ☐ **QE 19** ($17.99) Judith Brett *Relaxed & Comfortable*
- ☐ **QE 20** ($17.99) John Birmingham *A Time for War*
- ☐ **QE 21** ($17.99) Clive Hamilton *What's Left?*
- ☐ **QE 22** ($17.99) Amanda Lohrey *Voting for Jesus*
- ☐ **QE 23** ($17.99) Inga Clendinnen *The History Question*
- ☐ **QE 24** ($17.99) Robyn Davidson *No Fixed Address*
- ☐ **QE 25** ($17.99) Peter Hartcher *Bipolar Nation*
- ☐ **QE 26** ($17.99) David Marr *His Master's Voice*
- ☐ **QE 27** ($17.99) Ian Lowe *Reaction Time*
- ☐ **QE 28** ($17.99) Judith Brett *Exit Right*
- ☐ **QE 29** ($17.99) Anne Manne *Love & Money*
- ☐ **QE 30** ($17.99) Paul Toohey *Last Drinks*
- ☐ **QE 31** ($17.99) Tim Flannery *Now or Never*
- ☐ **QE 32** ($17.99) Kate Jennings *American Revolution*
- ☐ **QE 33** ($17.99) Guy Pearse *Quarry Vision*
- ☐ **QE 34** ($17.99) Annabel Crabb *Stop at Nothing*
- ☐ **QE 35** ($17.99) Noel Pearson *Radical Hope*
- ☐ **QE 36** ($17.99) Mungo MacCallum *Australian Story*
- ☐ **QE 37** ($17.99) Waleed Aly *What's Right?*
- ☐ **QE 38** ($17.99) David Marr *Power Trip*
- ☐ **QE 39** ($17.99) Hugh White *Power Shift*
- ☐ **QE 40** ($17.99) George Megalogenis *Trivial Pursuit*
- ☐ **QE 41** ($17.99) David Malouf *The Happy Life*
- ☐ **QE 42** ($17.99) Judith Brett *Fair Share*
- ☐ **QE 43** ($17.99) Robert Manne *Bad News*
- ☐ **QE 44** ($17.99) Andrew Charlton *Man-Made World*
- ☐ **QE 45** ($17.99) Anna Krien *Us and Them*
- ☐ **QE 46** ($17.99) Laura Tingle *Great Expectations*
- ☐ **QE 47** ($17.99) David Marr *Political Animal*
- ☐ **QE 48** ($17.99) Tim Flannery *After the Future*
- ☐ **QE 49** ($17.99) Mark Latham *Not Dead Yet*
- ☐ **QE 50** ($17.99) Anna Goldsworthy *Unfinished Business*
- ☐ **QE 51** ($17.99) David Marr *The Prince*
- ☐ **QE 52** ($17.99) Linda Jaivin *Found in Translation*
- ☐ **QE 53** ($17.99) Paul Toohey *That Sinking Feeling*
- ☐ **QE 54** ($17.99) Andrew Charlton *Dragon's Tail*
- ☐ **QE 55** ($17.99) Noel Pearson *A Rightful Place*
- ☐ **QE 56** ($17.99) Guy Rundle *Clivosaurus*
- ☐ **QE 57** ($17.99) Karen Hitchcock *Dear Life*
- ☐ **QE 58** ($17.99) David Kilcullen *Blood Year*
- ☐ **QE 59** ($17.99) David Marr *Faction Man*
- ☐ **QE 60** ($17.99) Laura Tingle *Political Amnesia*
- ☐ **QE 61** ($17.99) George Megalogenis *Balancing Act*
- ☐ **QE 62** ($17.99) James Brown *Firing Line*
- ☐ **QE 63** ($17.99) Don Watson *Enemy Within*
- ☐ **QE 64** ($17.99) Stan Grant *The Australian Dream*
- ☐ **QE 65** ($17.99) David Marr *The White Queen*
- ☐ **QE 66** ($17.99) Anna Krien *The Long Goodbye*
- ☐ **QE 67** ($17.99) Benjamin Law *Moral Panic 101*
- ☐ **QE 68** ($17.99) Hugh White *Without America*
- ☐ **QE 69** ($17.99) Mark McKenna *Moment of Truth*
- ☐ **QE 70** ($17.99) Richard Denniss *Dead Right*
- ☐ **QE 71** ($17.99) Laura Tingle *Follow the Leader*
- ☐ **QE 72** ($17.99) Sebastian Smee *Net Loss*
- ☐ **QE 73** ($17.99) Rebecca Huntley *Australia Fair*
- ☐ **QE 74** ($17.99) Erik Jensen *The Prosperity Gospel*
- ☐ **QE 75** ($17.99) Annabel Crabb *Men at Work*
- ☐ **QE 76** ($17.99) Peter Hartcher *Red Flag*
- ☐ **QE 77** ($17.99) Margaret Simons *Cry Me a River*
- ☐ **QE 78** ($17.99) Judith Brett *The Coal Curse*
- ☐ **QE 79** ($24.99) Katharine Murphy *The End of Certainty*
- ☐ **QE 80** ($24.99) Laura Tingle *The High Road*
- ☐ **QE 81** ($24.99) Alan Finkel *Getting to Zero*

Please include this form with delivery and payment details overleaf.
Back issues also available as eBooks at **quarterlyessay.com**